Six-Figure Shoeing

How to Build a Profitable and Rewarding Farrier Business

Doug Butler, PhD, CJF, FWCF

Six-Figure Shoeing

Edited by Barbara McNichol
Cover design and page layout by Karen Saunders
Printed by Walsworth Co., Inc.

Published by
Doug Butler Enterprises, Inc.
P.O. Box 1390
LaPorte, CO 80535
1-800-728-3826

ISBN 0-916992-20-10

Dedication

To our families,
whose love and support
make being in business
rewarding and worthwhile.

Table of Contents

Preface

Many people have been lured by the media into trying the farrier profession. But the combination of an uninformed public and inadequately trained practitioners has created all sorts of scenarios. In the same environment where opportunity abounds to make a six-figure income, incompetence runs rampant. A new horse owner selects a farrier almost entirely on the basis of availability and dependability. Personality overshadows craftsmanship. Competence is of little concern until an animal goes lame.

Nearly every report published about the farrier industry indicates that business management is the area most in need of improvement. This book was written to help increase the prosperity of self-motivated farriers in America. According to a survey of 627 farriers by the *American Farriers Journal* in 1998, full-time farriers averaged $55,723 gross income in a 50-week year. Ten percent of farriers in heavily populated areas bring in over $100,000 annually. Nationally, about 5% of farriers make over $100,000.

Anyone can improve his or her economic situation by simply paying more attention to business. Those farriers who work to make it a habit will be among the top 5% and become six-figure shoers! Many farriers who have business savvy in addition to craftsmanship skill have a unique advantage: a partnership. Often a farrier's greatest ally is a helpmate who manages the business. She or he should also read this book.

Highly skilled and service-oriented farriers are certainly in demand. Yet, for the best to remain available and dependable, they must also run a viable business. Today's economy has created an opportunity for farriers willing to work *on* their businesses as much as they work *in* them to make a six-figure income. This book shows you how.

Introduction

Today, owning horses is a choice, not a necessity. Farriers provide services to a hobby industry. As such, we are dispensable. Still, we must make business choices that create a perception of necessity and value in every client's mind. We have to master business skills, as well as mechanical skills, if we want to be successful.

I wrote this book after four years of interviews and surveys combined with 40 years of experience in the farrier industry. This includes 30 years of teaching farrier training courses. The examples and techniques discussed reflect the career path and methods of the leaders in our industry. I believe that observing people who are doing what they want to do, then practicing their techniques until habits are formed, is the best way to duplicate and even surpass the success of others.

There have been no standards of success developed formally to stimulate skill improvements in the farrier world. This is partly due to a lack of mandatory board certification so prevalent in other pro-fessions, and partly due to a lack of motivation on the part of farriers to raise their own skill levels.

Farriers and veterinarians have the same roots. For some time after separating into distinct specialties, animosity and jealousy prevailed. A certain amount of this still exists. I believe it primarily originates from an unclear definition of roles and a reluctance to understand each other's professions. When ego and pride get in the way, the value of each other's experience gets discounted. Clearly, both professions are needed to help expensive, marginally sound horses give their optimum performances.

Traditionally, farriers learned their trade in apprenticeships. Indenture was often a part of the training agreement in Europe. Apprentices promised – under threat of severe penalties and even death – not to share the details of the training they received with anyone. The apprentice functioned nearly as slave labor for his master for an extended period of time, ranging from four to eleven years, with the average being seven.

American tradesmen reduced the time and severity of the apprenticeship experience by establishing short courses or "schools" of a few months to a few years in length. After training, it was up to the graduates to establish their own independent businesses. This was a difficult step and many failed. As horse numbers declined during the first half of the 20th century, some blacksmiths adapted their skills to take care of automobiles. Others went out of business. Farrier schools came back in the second half of the century with an all-time high of 100 in 1975. Today, approximately 40 courses are offered in the United States. They vary tremendously in length and quality.

Attending a farrier course or school is just the beginning. Continuing education through clinics and seminars is the most popular way to learn the trade today. Self-education through home study courses, including books and videos, is practiced by the most successful farriers. Farriery, as with any trade, is best learned one-on-one. Personal coaching, sometimes called mentoring, is the fastest way to make significant progress and advance to the next level in your farrier career. Choose your mentor wisely.

Building a career is like putting up a building. You must construct a sound foundation from knowledge and experience before you build a superstructure of loyal, satisfied clients on top of it. There is a tendency to build too fast in the farrier business. When it catches up to you, you can become frustrated with your own awkwardness when trying to perform at higher levels than you are prepared for. A weak foundation due to poor mastery of the basics will eventually cause your career to fall apart. This book helps you understand and commit to mastering the business.

Successful people set goals. They know where they are going and imagine how they will get there. They visualize the entire process, then break it down into achievable steps. They are willing to study, practice and take risks to achieve their goals. This book also helps successful people get the results they desire and deserve.

The format of this book follows that of a business plan. I have included ideas and examples that have worked for me and others. If you study, plan and apply these ideas, you will reach your goals and earn a six-figure income.

How do you build a profitable and rewarding farrier business? You get grounded, get focused, get organized, get customers, get successful and get balanced. Get going and good luck!

Doug Butler
February, 2001

Chapter 1

The Farrier Business

Chapter 1

The Farrier Business

Definition

The dictionary defines a farrier as one who shoes horses. Horseshoeing looks deceptively easy when done by someone who is skilled, but it is very difficult to do accurately and efficiently. It is even harder to build and maintain a sustainable farrier business.

In ancient times, "farrier" had other meanings, including what we would today call a veterinary technician. In fact, the veterinary profession grew out of the farrier profession. The two trades have been separate for less than 200 years.

Requirements

Few professions demand as much mental and physical effort as farriery. A high level of horsemanship and physical stamina are expected. However, the reason most farriers miss being financially successful is not due to lack of horsemanship or ironworking skill; rather, they lack business skill.

I have worked in the farrier industry for over four decades. In that time, I have seen a lot of people start their farrier business and fizzle out after a couple of years. Less than 5% of all American farriers are still in the farrier business full time after five years. As an industry, we have focused so much on the technical aspects of farriery that we have neglected the critical principles of strategic planning and business management.

People get into the farrier business for many reasons. Feeling involved in meaningful work is one of those reasons. It doesn't matter why you decide to get into farriery; what matters is that it is meaningful to you. Learning about the heritage of your chosen profession is one way to find meaning.

Heritage

Here, we discuss the heritage of farriery as it comes to the United States from Great Britain, or the United Kingdom. Other countries also have a rich heritage, but few have progressed as far or influenced Americans as much as the English heritage.

The term "farrier" came into general use in England around 1562 A.D. (according to Worshipful Company of Farriers [WCF] tradition). It is from the old French, *ferrier*, and Latin, *ferrarius*, which is from *ferrum*, meaning "horseshoe." Before this, persons who shod horses were called "marshalls." In fact, the forefathers of the Worshipful Company of Farriers during the time of Edward III established "the Marshalls of the City of London" in 1356 A.D. by the Court of the Mayor and Alderman of the City of London. The organization was re-established by petitioning King Charles II in 1674, since most of the records of the city of London were lost in the Great Fire of 1666.

The Worshipful Company of Farriers (WCF) was number 55 in order of precedence as one of the London Livery (Elected Voters) Companies. The stated original purpose of the WCF was to set standards of workmanship and provide proper training to protect the kingdom against the damage done by "unexpert and unskilled persons." "Persons exercising the art and mistery of the Farryer within the area (7 mile radius of London city) should demean and behave themselves in all matters appertaining to the said Art of Mistery of a Farryer. Unless [one] had served as an Apprentice to the said trade for *seven years*, upon such penalties can be inflicted for contempt of our Royal will and pleasure." This was done accord-

ing to Prince (1980) in his book *The Farrier and His Craft* "at the request of Several Nobleman and Gentlemen of the First Distinction who have suffered by the Ignorance of unskilled Quacks who assume to themselves the name of Farriers."

Later, voluntary competency qualification examinations were established, and finally the Farrier Registration Act was passed by Parliament as an animal welfare act in this progression: RSS (1890) [later DWCF (1975)], AFCL (1890) [later AWCF (1975)], and FWCF (1890).

George Fleming, in dedicating his classic 1869 book, *Horseshoes and Horseshoeing*, said about horseshoeing, [it is] ". . . an art which kings and nobles have not disdained to study and practice, and which is very intimately connected with the comfort and utility of the noblest and most useful animal ever domesticated by man . . ."

Historically, farriers were not only horseshoers but were also concerned with the treatment of the general ailments of horses, and thence with other animals. As noted in Prince's *The Farrier and His Craft*, Captain William Burdon, writing in 1732, stated that "a farrier is as useful a trade as any other in His Majesty's Dominion; we commonly call him Doctor because he professes Physick and Surgery among horses; and some are good and sensible men . . ."

The farrier was superseded by the college-trained veterinary surgeon during the 19th century. These "surgeons" evolved into equine physicians and practitioners of preventative medicine. "Ignorant and unskillful quacks who assume to themselves the name of farrier" did great damage, especially with regard to medications. In fact, it has been noted that even until just a few years ago, traditional quack farrier medicines were still available in the U.K. Firing (burning holes or lines in the flesh) has only recently been declared barbaric and ineffectual in the U.S. It is still widely practiced in many parts of the world.

Farriers were masters of powerful and frightening things – fire, horses, iron and sharp tools. In early years, farriery was associated with magic and the supernatural. Farriers thought to have special powers and were highly regarded in their communities.

A distinguishing feature of the ancient guilds included oaths of secrecy. An example of an oath of secrecy is the Horseman's Oath, a copy of which I obtained on my last trip to England. There were severe penalties for those who wrote or

> *Farriers were masters of powerful and frightening things – fire, horses, iron and sharp tools.*

spoke of any part of the "true horsemanship" that must be "concealed and never revealed." The idea was to limit knowledge to protect oneself and one's community.

Our civilization, and especially our trade, has come a long way in this area. I can still remember some of the farriers I observed in my youth who were unwilling to share their secrets with anyone.

THE HORSEMAN'S OATH

I of my own free will and accord solemnly vow and swear before God and all these witnesses that I will heal, conceal, and never reveal any part of the true horsemanship which I am about to receive at this time. Furthermore, I solemnly vow and swear that I will neither write it nor indite, cut it nor carve it on wood or stone, nor yet on anything moveable or immoveable under the canopy of heaven, nor yet so much as wave a finger in the air to none but a horseman.

Furthermore, I vow and swear that I will never give it nor see it given to a tradesman of any kind except to a blacksmith or a veterinary surgeon or a horse-soldier. Furthermore, I will never give it nor see it given to a farmer or a farmer's son unless he be working his own or his father's horses. Furthermore, I will never give it nor see it given to a fool nor a madman nor to my father nor mother nor brother nor to any womankind. Furthermore I will never give it nor see it given to my wife nor daughter nor yet to the very dearest ever to lay by my side.

Furthermore, I will never give it nor see it given to anyone after sunset on Saturday night nor before sunrise on Monday morning. Furthermore, I will neither abuse nor bad use any man's horses with it and if I see a brother do so I will tell him of his fault. Furthermore, I will never advise anyone to get it nor disadvise anyone from getting it but leave every one to his own free will and accord. Furthermore, I will never give it nor see it given to any under the age of sixteen nor above the age of forty-five. Furthermore, I will never give it nor see it given unless there be three or more lawful sworn brethren present after finding them to be so by trying and examining them. Furthermore, I will never give it or see it given for less than the sum of £1 sterling or the value thereof. Furthermore, I will never refuse to attend a meeting if warned within three days except in a case of riding fire or going for the doctor, and if I fail to keep these promises may my flesh be torn to pieces with a wild horse and my heart cut through with a horseman's knife and my

bones buried on the sands of the seashore where the tide ebbs and flows every twenty-four hours so that there may be no remembrance of me amongst lawful brethren so help me God to keep these promises. Amen.

Author's History

I obtained my first horseshoeing book while in junior high school. It was *The Principles and Practice of Horseshoeing* by Charles M. Holmes, FWCF. Reading the book inspired me. In 1980, I met David Gulley, FWCF, and David Duckett, FWCF. I admired their skills. I obtained permission to take the WCF examinations in 1986 as a result of my second trip to the United Kingdom as a North American Horseshoeing Team member. I passed the DWCF in 1987, the AWCF in 1989, and the FWCF in 1992. This is, by far, my greatest professional achievement to date. My examination for earning my Ph.D. at Cornell University was difficult, but it pales in comparison with that of the FWCF exam. I became only the 150th person to pass the examination in the history of the Worshipful Company of Farriers.

Training

Having taught the skill of farriery for nearly 40 years, I am repeatedly amazed at how each new group of students must start at the same place. They must work just as hard as the previous group to make progress. Students who are physically fit and have some experience in the use of tools for construction and manual or farm labor usually learn the fastest. The skill of farriery appears deceptively simple to the observer, but is, in fact, very complex and takes many years to learn. In addition to the physical requirement, successful farriers have aptitude in biology, biomechanics and business. There are no short cuts. Those who have "skipped grades" when learning have had to go back and pick up the training they missed before they could really progress in their careers.

Proclus, the ancient Greek philosopher, tells the story of the fascination that Ptolemy I, Egypt's pharaoh in 300 B.C., had with geometry. Ptolemy invited Euclid, the Greek mathematician who was called even then "the father of geometry," to teach him. After a short time, Ptolemy told Euclid that the process of studying geometry was too slow. He declared, "I'm not like your other students. You must have a quicker, shorter method for teaching geometry to a pharaoh." In response, Euclid

Euclid gave voice to a principle that can be said of horseshoeing, "Your Majesty, there is no royal road to geometry!"

gave voice to a principle that can be said of horseshoeing, "Your Majesty, there is no royal road to geometry!"

I have also learned through a lifetime of experience there is no royal road to learning the art and mystery of the farrier. However, there *is* a road, and it is clearly marked. It is a difficult road and, like any road to success, it is paved with exertions rather than intentions. Earl Nightingale once said, "An hour of study a day on a given subject will make a person a foremost expert in five years." That's why it's important to commit to continual learning and recognize some judgment is required to travel this road. Good judgment is obtained by experience; ironically experience often comes from poor judgment.

Challenging oneself with competition against the clock generally speeds the progression of skill learning. I have had a love affair with horseshoeing and have learned the value of preparation for competition. In observing many great farriers and many want-to-be farriers in my life, I have learned that determination and willingness to build on an honest assessment of where one really is often accelerates progress.

The most difficult thing to assess when teaching farriery is the *level* of determination of the student. The most difficult skill to teach to the uninitiated is applied horse behavior or horsemanship. And the most valuable prerequisite seems to be a successful self-employment experience that requires dealing with the public.

Perhaps farrier training is best taught in modules. This requires a student to intensely study a subject as a unit, then write practice competency exams over each unit as it is completed. Using this system, learning is arranged in a sequence so a student qualifies by official examination in one competency before being examined in another. There are eight of these learning modules in the pre-farriery courses in the U.K. Each works toward fulfilling requirements for National Vocational Qualifications (NVQ) in the U.K. farrier training system. NVQs are committee-specified standards based on work performance, not learning or training performance.

There has been no formalized farrier training system in America. Farriery is unregulated here, perhaps as it should be. It means that the decision to select

Farriery is unregulated here, perhaps as it should be. It means that the decision to select a farrier is solely made by the horse owner and not by governmental agencies.

a farrier is solely made by the horse owner and not by governmental agencies.

Honesty

There is no room for pretending in the farrier business. Either you can do it or you can't. Supervised rote practice is necessary to develop skill.

When assessing competence, time limits and precision specifications must be established because skill equals accuracy plus speed.

Skill = Accuracy + Speed

Becoming a competent farrier is much like learning to play a piano. Only rarely can persons (called virtuosos) master the instrument by themselves. To truly master an instrument like the piano or a hammer is a lifetime quest. It follows that we must learn from a master if we wish to play a symphony. There are 88 keys on the piano but thousands of symphonies. You recognize, as a fact of life, that few persons will ever play a symphony (except on a CD player) and fewer still will ever write a symphony. There always has been, and there always will be, plenty of room at the top in this field.

Instruction from a qualified expert is important. But probably more important are the your own character attributes, including a willingness to learn and honestly represent your own desires.

Inherent Qualities

The following inherent qualities are recognized by horseshoeing school instructors as the principal characteristics a successful student – and experienced farrier – must possess. The statements under each category are arranged in this order: things one likes to do, things one is committed to do, and things one can do. The "can do's" must be present; the others can be developed.

Horse sense

A good farrier:
- Appreciates the elegance, athletic ability and capability (danger) of horses.
- Commits to the humane care and treatment of horses.
- Can read and work a horse with patience – is unafraid of horses.

Business sense

A good farrier:
- Is financially motivated.

- Commits to piecework (versus salary) and working alone.
- Enjoys hard work and being self-reliant.

Mechanical sense

A good farrier:
- Likes to work with hands and tools – unafraid of fire.
- Commits to creative craftwork – takes pride in work.
- Has eye-hand coordination, manual dexterity and rhythm.

Artistic sense

A good farrier:
- Has a sense of form and proportion.
- Has ability to visualize a process and the end product.
- Uses creative imagination and drawing skills.

People sense

A good farrier:
- Is courteous and considerate of others.
- Commits to communication or liaison between concerned horse people.
- Has a service-orientation toward paying clients.

Science sense

A good farrier:

- Appreciates working on a living animal.

- Commits to the study of the structure and function of the horse and its foot.

- Studies basic sciences including anatomy, physiology, pathology, biomechanics.

- Knows behavioral science as a helpful addition to the work.

Physical fitness

A good farrier:

- Is free of limiting physical and learning disabilities.

- Enjoys physical stimulation of muscles and has high pain tolerance.

- Is physically fit as determined by medical examination.

Personal responsibility

A good farrier:

- Has a teachable attitude, including a willingness to learn.

- Commits to paying the price of life-long learning, including apprenticeships, schools, conferences and clinics.

- Possesses good judgment and common sense (insurance coverage, personal grooming, life balance, etc.).

Distinguishing Points

Over the years, I have interviewed many successful farriers making a six-figure income. What distinguishes these highly successful farriers from all others? Here are the seven reasons that were most apparent.

1. Successful farriers have **a strong desire to be successful**, combined with faith in their own ability. Driven with a desire to achieve, they are not afraid of hard work and would do whatever it takes to reach their goals. As competent horsemen, they have a lifetime of experience riding and working with all types of horses. Above all, they enjoy working with their hands and making things.

2. Successful farriers have **obtained a solid foundation of skill training** from a master of the craft. In recognizing a standard of excellence, they have a deep desire to achieve that standard. They are constantly engaged in practice of their skills as if seeking to master a musical instrument. They faithfully made the most of their schooling and learning experiences. They are honest about their level of experience. Their willingness to learn new skills continues.

3. Successful farriers **continually grow and improve** by seeking out educational opportunities. This includes studying from textbooks, then applying concepts. They recognize the importance of an hour a day of diligent study, which leads to expert status in a few years. Improvement takes the form of regularly listening to audiotapes while driving to clients' homes and viewing videos on a wide range of horseshoeing subjects at every opportunity. In addition to reading trade magazines, they frequently attend clinics and workshops, applying what they learned on a daily basis. They practice their skill techniques until they can produce with confidence under pressure. Many establish a weekly practice time, often with another farrier.

4. Successful farriers **record their successes** on film and in writing, sharing them with clients and fellow professionals. They keep pictures and stories of representative cases in notebook form in their vehicles for ready reference. As well, they make videos of important representative cases and collect charts, specimens and shoes to illustrate important concepts. They make a practice of sharing articles of interest with their clients. Often they give their clients educational materials in the form of booklets, charts, tapes, hoof picks, etc.

5. Successful farriers **continue to sell themselves** with enthusiasm every day, on the job and off. By stressing the *value* of their work, not the price, they position themselves as educators and experts in their field. They continually show consideration regarding their clients' time and property, thus building loyalty by providing excellent service.

6. Successful farriers **present a professional image** with each client contact. Attentive to personal grooming and clothes, they drive trucks that are clean, organized, well stocked and maintained. They first assess a job, give an estimate and then apply the assessment fee to the job. They hand out brochures listing their business and referral policies. They present an itemized bill with work, materials, travel and consulting fees clearly listed. Keeping their calendars on hand for scheduling and reminder calls, they make it a rule to reach appointments at the time scheduled, or to call ahead to communicate any delay. They use a contact management system or data base such as computer software, index cards or appointment books to stay organized.

7. Successful farriers **have goals for their various roles** in their work and in their lives. They run their businesses like businesses, knowing their costs, profits and bottom line each month. That means they seek ways to in-

crease their income by obtaining more clients, raising prices and/or cutting costs. They also strive to manage their time wisely, scheduling everything, including personal time. Consistently, they set and achieve realistic, long-term and short-term goals.

Every technique won't work for every person. But the more of these behaviors you can apply in your own business, the more successful it will be.

Animal Rights Issue

We live in a society in which less than 1% of the population lives on farms and less than 10% of our income is spent on food. This is a testimony of the great efficiency of the American farmer. Few people understand or even care where their food comes from. Farriers are challenged daily by the ignorance that comes from people disconnected from the land and the animals that once powered the traditional farm.

There are still a large number of horses used on ranches in the Western U.S. However, most of these are cared for exclusively by the owners or ranch help. These horses form a separate community from those that most horseshoers service.

Farriers often see horses whose owners place impossible expectations on them. We are asked questions that can't be answered and are expected to solve problems that can't be solved. We are placed in the difficult position of serving two masters: the one who employs us, and the one who is silent but whose needs we are duty-bound to address. In one sense, we are paid to care, but in another sense, it is caring that really pays our "satisfaction wage."

The vast majority of people in our affluent American society (over 80% by some surveys) believe that animals have rights. In the U.S., there are more than 400 animal rights organizations, many with an aggressive agenda for influencing public opinion. The real question is, how far do these rights extend? The parameters keep changing. On one end of the scale, liberationists believe horses should not be ridden or produce any benefit for man. On the other end, exploitationists believe horses don't perceive pain as we do, and it is acceptable to cause animals to suffer or to kill them for sport. Horse professionals cannot endorse either extreme position.

In reality, the opinions of most horse professionals fall in the middle, advocating animal use *and* animal welfare. They believe animals are here for human use and enjoyment, but they have a responsibility to make them comfortable and spare them suffering, if possible.

Farriers have several responsibilities in this emotional-charged environment. Our principal duty is to provide the best service we can with the intent of preventing suffering. We must take our role seriously as strong advocates for animal welfare. We do this by giving common-sense guidance to an animal-use-ignorant society that changes its consensus due to the influences of a well-financed, well-organized and vocal animal rights movement.

It has been my experience that most of the unnecessary suffering we see in horses stems from ignorant neglect rather than intentional cruelty. Some people buy horses before they realize the responsibility that goes with them. A lot of problems simply result from inattention to their animals due to preoccupation with a busy, crazy and even frantic world.

When dealing with cases of animal "abuse" or cruelty, we must

On one end of the scale, liberationists believe horses should not be ridden or produce any benefit for man. On the other end, exploitationists believe horses don't perceive pain as we do, and it is acceptable to cause animals to suffer or to kill them for sport. Horse professionals cannot endorse either extreme position.

carefully weigh our role as farriers. We must also recognize that people apply different standards of care that make very little difference to the horse, as it is a hardy creature of habit.

In each situation, ask yourself if the various standards of horse care you observe are causing the animal suffering. Remember, *too much* attention to "comfort" may be as bad or worse than *too little*. For example, an animal that is overmedicated and kept in a poorly ventilated stall may be less resistant to disease than one left to fend for itself in a pasture.

If you choose to become involved in a welfare case as a farrier, be sure to document your monitoring of the situation and all conversations you have had. This is because you may be asked or even required to testify in a courtroom trial. Also be prepared for your involvement to alienate you from the offending horse owner and his or her friends.

Chapter 2

Challenges and Opportunities in the Farrier Business

Chapter 2

Challenges and Opportunities in the Farrier Business

State of America's Horse Industry

A 1998 study conducted by the National Agricultural Statistics Service (NASS) estimated there are 5.25 million horses in the U.S. This is down from the 6.9 million estimated by the American Horse Council (AHC) study a few years before. The AHC's study is thought to be the more accurate one because it was based on 725,000 surveys while the NASS was based on 20,000.

Horse numbers have gone up from an all-time low of 2.5 million in 1960 to as many as 10 million in the early 1980s. Since then, numbers have gone down. The Tax Reform Act of 1986 was especially responsible for reducing the number of expensive horses kept for tax deduction/evasion purposes. It is interesting to note that, in America, more than 60% of all income taxes are paid by 5% of the taxpayers.

Today's horses, though, are fewer in number, are owned by more individuals who spend more money on a horse for their purchase and care more than ever before. Some studies indicate a high turnover rate for horse owners; only about 10% keep a horse for more than three years. About one-tenth of the nation's horses are sold each year. In 1998, horse sales amounted to $1.75 billion.

About 7 million people are considered stakeholders in the horse industry, with about 2 million people actually owning the horses. Tens of millions more participate as spectators at horse events of (around 270 million people in the U.S. in 1998). Surveys by horse youth organizations show that one-third of U.S. households are potentially able to own and/or ride horses.

People are keeping horses longer and spending more on feed and services to maintain them than ever before. Nearly one-half of all horses are used for pleasure riding. About one-tenth of America's horses are used for racing, one-fourth for showing and one-sixth for farm and ranch work, rodeo and police work.

Statistics show that people who own horses can afford them

and typically are not in the business to make money with their horses. The median income for all horse-owning households is $60,000 compared to $36,000 for all U.S. households. Only 14% of horse owning households have incomes under $25,000. Studies show that less than 25% of horse owners' total annual income is from horse activities.

A recent study in Texas showed that horse owners spend about 35% of the average purchase price of a horse annually for its care. The average cost of the horses studied was $5,249 while the average cost of their care was $1,849 annually. Horse owners spend about 45% of horse care expenses for feed. About 15% of horse care expense is for hoof care. This percentage is less in areas where feed and boarding costs are higher. Specifically, *Equus* magazine reported this percentage at 7% in the Northeast a few years ago, and Colorado's horse industry survey put it at 10%. Veterinary care expense is often less than farrier expense unless emergency care is needed. Certainly, the farrier interacts with the owner more often that the vet does due to the necessity of eight-week (or less) intervals for hoof care.

The most common reasons people give for spending money on horse maintenance are recreation and relaxation to reduce stress.

The most common reasons people give for spending money on horse maintenance are recreation and relaxation to reduce stress. Its value in promoting character training in children is frequently mentioned. The challenge of competition is also considered important. People spend about $25.36 billion annually for goods and services for their horses; the total impact of the horse industry on the U.S. economy is estimated by the AHC to be $112 billion a year.

Challenges Facing Horse Owners

Farriers need to be aware of issues that affect horse owners' ability to keep horses. Many areas have become "unfriendly" to horses due to the passing of legislation sponsored by non-agricultural neighbors. This has forced many boarding stables out of business. Land use zoning, water use, acreage minimums, trail closings, manure disposal, as well as unfavorable "attractive nuisance" and "liability" ordinances, all threaten horse ownership and use.

Recently, legislation changing the classification of horses from agricultural to pet status has been proposed in several states. This is very harmful to horse owners. It is especially for landowners who face their tax base changing from agricultural to residential. This results in a significant increase in taxes. Already, it is illegal to send horses to slaughter in one state because they are classified as pets and non-agricultural commodities. This raises significant disposal and humane issues.

State of the Farrier Industry

Various estimates have been given for the number of farriers in the U.S. Since many are part-time, an accurate figure is difficult to obtain. Published estimates range from 10,000 to 50,000. The *American Farriers Journal* estimated 27,500 full- and part-time shoers in the U.S. in 1999. The American Farriers Association (AFA) has about 2,600 members. About 10% of farriers are women. And many farriers don't belong to farrier organizations – they simply are not joiners.

A full-time farrier services 250 to 300 horses a year if they are cared for regularly (every eight weeks). Numbers may be higher when the shoeing interval is longer. Part-time farriers' numbers will be more variable than these, depending on the nature of their businesses.

Farrier preparation and training varies tremendously throughout this country.

A report from the U.K. (Feb. 2000) indicated there were 570,650 horses with 2,300 registered farriers in the British Isles. The Farriers Registration Council estimated that the average farrier has 277 horses on their books. The average farrier earns £15,500 per year or about $27,000 – about half what the average American farrier makes.

There are 595 companies manufacturing and supplying products for farriers in America who use nearly 24,000 different products for horse foot care. Nearly 90% of farriers buy from retailers; only about 25% buy from manufacturers while 33% buy from wholesalers.

Farrier preparation and training varies tremendously throughout this country. According to the *American Farriers Journal* (AFJ), about 75% of farriers have attended one of the 40 training schools in the U.S. About 50% have worked as apprentices for an average of two years. About twice as many (70%) attend continuing education clinics as attend seminars, workshops or competitions (35%). Approximately 90 clinicians present to farrier groups. Most farriers have a high school diploma (96%) and a majority have had some college training. About

20% have a bachelor's degree, 5% a masters and 1% a doctorate.

Career longevity may be comparatively short for farriers because they should expect to spend 20 to 30 years working to reach any degree of success. Of those attending farrier school, only 5 to 10% stay in the business full time after five years. The majority is between 40 and 59 years of age while less than 5% are over 60. About 40% are under 40.

Full-time farriers average 31 horses shod in a 45-hour week. Many spend longer hours due to travel and inefficiency. Farriers travel an average of 472 miles per week, as 98% of farriers work from a mobile shop. Only 15% charge mileage expenses to their customers. Most farriers have medical insurance (78%), while 33% carry disability and only 20% carry liability insurance. About 25% of farriers have no retirement plan while 40% of full-time farriers earn income from other sources.

Farriers in the Northeast and Far West gross about $10,000 more per year than those in the Midwest, Southeast and West. The average American full-time farrier grossed $55,723 in 1998. This is based on the assumption that the farrier worked on 1,550 horses in a 50-week year (at a rate of 31 per week).

However, about 10% of farriers gross over $100,000. These are six-figure shoers! The difference is usually a function of how much time they are willing to spend working *on* their business – not how much time they work *in* their business.

Opportunities Facing Farriers

This industry presents an opportunity for highly motivated, well-trained and dedicated farriers to make an income comparable with most professionals. The farrier's job has a low entrance cost but a high continuing education and maintenance cost. The national average for beginning veterinarians' and lawyers' salaries is below the national average for farriers.

Farrier work is physical; it is dirty, smelly and dangerous – all of those things your mother told you to stay away from. But it can be profitable and rewarding. If you make a go of it, even the most skeptical parent will be proud of you! I know this from personal experience.

Farriers are seen by clients in light of their past experience. Farriers may be perceived as ignorant, arrogant, crude, rude, armstrong, head-strong and indulgent. One must overcome these perceptions to be successful in a competitive business. Modern clients value promptness, integrity, horse knowledge, cleanliness and courtesy, as well as skill in the craft.

Farriers practicing in areas where their horse owners have little or no selection may never know how they are regarded. They must remember that since this is a service profession to a hobby industry, they are dispensable. Farriers must choose to position themselves as desirable partners to support the clients' love of horses. They must contribute to the peace and relaxation clients expect to get from their horses. They must master more than the mere mechanical skills of their profession.

> *They must contribute to the peace and relaxation clients expect to get from their horses.*

Training As A Challenge

Farriery is best learned one-on-one. For centuries, the time-honored way to learn this and any other craft has been through apprenticeship. The agreements were very specific and amounted to what we today would call a non-competitive, non-disclosure agreement. Apprentices worked with master farriers and sequentially learned skills at different levels. The master farrier would not permit the apprentice to perform the more advanced procedures until it was obvious that the apprentice had consistently mastered the basic concepts and could apply them to a wide variety of situations. Through his own practice and ap-

plying the experience of others, the apprentice could move up through the levels of the craft to likewise become a master.

In today's enlightened society, it seems we would still strongly adhere to such a system. However, due to the demands made on unskilled farriers by an unknowledgable public, incompetence has been able to thrive. Uneducated horse owners hire incompetent individuals who have not mastered their trade to do therapeutic work on horses with serious ailments. These unskilled farriers frequently create a bad reputation for the profession.

Unlike most trades, farriery does not currently require certification to practice. Doctors, dentists, veterinarians, lawyers and even hairdressers require some kind of state certification to be able to practice. When doctors go to school, they learn various principles and techniques they can employ in surgery or medicinal practices. Doctors in training spend months and even years simulating the actual operation before they are permitted to cut into living flesh. They must prove their competence at a lower level before they are permitted to operate on a higher level.

Unfortunately, many American farriers practice above their skill level. This is due in part to a noneducated horseowning public who can't recognize the skill of a competent farrier. It is also due to the fact that many farriers are not capable of recognizing their weaknesses and actual skill level. When farriers practice at a higher skill level than they have earned, they eventually will be found out, often to the detriment of their business.

Today, owners spend more money on their horses but pay less attention to them than in earlier decades. Many horses are not fully trained and have especially poor ground manners. As a whole, owner skill with horses is decreasing in spite of an increase in equine clinicians. It seems that all the horse whispering isn't loud enough!

In addition, horses are being bred with conformation defects that predispose to unsoundness. Soundness is being overlooked in favor of color, disposition and tractability (ability to be easily trained). As a result, many of our modern horses will require expert farrier care all of their lives.

People are keeping horses longer and, therefore, spending more dollars on each horse. That means our liability exposure is greater than ever due to today's litigation-happy climate. Fortunately, liability insurance and protection is easier to obtain than it once was.

Our Biggest Challenge

Perhaps our biggest challenge is dealing with the myriad of fads or "novelties" that permeate our industry. They are so well advertised and promoted that it is difficult to warn clients of their folly (until they have a bad experience). Deception and "con" persons can flourish when people are ignorant of the fundamentals.

A product or technique (and its promoters) should be evaluated thoroughly before embracing and endorsing it (them) to your clients. If you don't, you may be placed in an embarrassing situation later on.

Before taking action, ask yourself these five questions:

1. Has the product or technique been subjected to *reliable research*? Or are the claims made based on unsupported testimonials?

2. Does the product or technique offer a *sensible*

When farriers practice at a higher skill level than they have earned, they eventually will be found out, often to the detriment of their business.

solution? Or is it sensational and positioned as "the only way" with those who don't accept it being labeled as "close-minded" or "old-fashioned?"

3. Does the developer/promoter have *credible credentials* and experience? Or has the developer/promoter avoided paying the price to be a legitimate solution provider?

4. Does the product or technique make *consistent claims* that hold up under close scrutiny? Or does it only work under special conditions and in the hands of the promoter?

5. Does the product or technique have *complete congruency* with proven traditional principles? Or is it promoted as a substitute for skill?

> *Horse persons, and especially farriers, are quick to fall for the divisive idea that we must embrace either tradition or technology. True professionals know that both tradition and technology are needed for success.*

Horse persons, and especially farriers, are quick to fall for the divisive idea that we must embrace either tradition or technology. True professionals know that both tradition and technology are needed for success.

As farriers, we have the opportunity to focus our efforts on acquiring sound principles and reliable techniques that allow us to consistently benefit the horse. That includes exposing current fads such as the "natural" fad.

Calling something natural is not necessarily good. As Frederick Remington, a great western artist said, "Nature is not kind. Indeed, she is merciless." Horses are better off domesticated than out in the wild fending for themselves.

Skilled farriers have improved the horse's life in this world. Breeding unsound horses and over-selection for a particular trait that is in fashion have caused many of the challenges we face today – not the domestication of the horse or the act of traditional horseshoeing by skilled farriers.

Chapter 3

Future Prospects
in the Farrier Business

Chapter 3

Future Prospects in the Farrier Business

Running A Farrier Business

What the future holds is anyone's guess. Today's most effective farriers are doing what all successful farriers will be doing in the future: paying as much attention to running their businesses as they do to balancing the horses' feet.

We will see fewer horses in the future, but the number of serious horse owners will increase. The more that people are separated from agriculture by a materialistic and mechanistic economy, the more attractive associating with live animals will become. With increased time and resources, those who have an unsatisfied craving for being around horses are likely to own them.

Horses will continue to be attractive to the upscale worker in those areas of the country where horse keeping is accepted and encouraged. Some communities and states are "horse friendly" and some are not. Owning horses is often attractive to those in "high-tech, low-touch" jobs. For these people, horses can provide a "safer" relationship than humans do, since horses require less emotional effort to build bonds.

Over time, the physical effort necessary to care for and shoe their horses will be even less desirable for many owners to consider doing it themselves. As a result, owners can expect to pay for expensive specialists that bring years of experience to the moment.

Having unknowledgeable clientele can be a two-edged sword for horse care providers such as farriers because they often have unrealistic expectations for their animals. In addition, their superficial level of knowledge of horsemanship and horseshoeing can make communication difficult and satisfaction hard to obtain.

Having unknowledgeable clientele can be a two-edged sword for horse care providers such as farriers because they often have unrealistic expectations for their animals.

For example, a client with unrealistic expectations often becomes deeply attached to a marginally sound horse and is unwilling to accept its limitations. However, this challenge can also be a great opportunity. Owners can develop dependence on, and trust in, the skilled, thoughtful farrier who makes an effort to educate and partner with them. Horses will be kept longer by single owners, usually until their deaths, and treated as members of the family rather than working partners.

Balancing Knowledge and Skill

A wise farrier will be prepared to be a *teacher* who balances knowledge and skill. The successful farrier of the future will be skilled in at least seven areas. The first letter of each of these areas spells TEACHER – Tradition, Ethics, Athletics, Craftsmanship, Horsemanship, Entrepreneurship and Recreation.

T - Tradition

The visual and mechanical skills necessary to practice good farriery have changed very little in hundreds of years. However, each generation has standards of acceptability created by the knowledge level of the clients and farriers. The speed of learning new material will continue to accelerate due to the widespread availability of learning experiences and materials. Learning strictly by trial and error will become a thing of the past.

The farrier industry is polarized now and will continue to be so. On the one hand, we have skilled professionals who have paid the price. On the other hand, we have charlatan pretenders who con the public. Con artists are only successful when the public is naïve and uninformed.

Constant vigilance will be required to prevent government regulation. If licensing or "registration" would improve our standard of performance, we should support it. However, little evidence exists to indicate that will happen. Improvement comes from pressure created through inside, not outside, influences. That is why legislated regulation of farriers won't improve the overall standard of practice. Rather, we all need to improve and constantly strive to better understand our craft. It is a life-time quest to master this, "the Master Craft."

Future farriers may have less need to practice the traditional skills of blacksmithing and shoemaking in front of the client due to wide availability and selection of every conceivable style of premade shoes. But farriers must practice these skills if they want to progress up the skill ladder.

Using high-tech products on feet prepared with low-tech skill and limited understanding will always be a disaster – both now and in the future. More training and practice with a skilled mentor will be valuable and even necessary for success. For these reasons, long distance life coaching, as well as skill coaching by phone or Internet, will become more popular.

High-tech everything has its advantages and disadvantages. Advantages come in the form of more efficient work, which should increase a person's effectiveness. The disadvantages are that it often doesn't. People still have to learn to use new technologies well. And they face a "common sense" learning curve as well as a "techy" learning curve.

Many people report that as they become more electronically connected, they seem to feel more disconnected and lonely. More people than ever before are working out of home offices. That's why, when farriers do their job, they need to make it a point to visit with people and build a human relationship at the same time they perform their technical function. In the future, people will value the experience of having the horse shod more than they ever have before because of this human connection.

> *Using high-tech products on feet prepared with low-tech skill and limited understanding will always be a disaster – both now and in the future.*

Clients will expect evaluations of products and techniques from the farrier they work with. The Internet and popular horse magazines will continue to be a source of misinformation for horse owners and will need to be addressed by knowledgeable farriers. More farriers will use web sites to communicate with their clients. In addition, a higher level of academic education, as well as longer practical skill training, will be required in the future to position farriers favorably among competitors in any given geographical area.

E - Ethics

The character of the farrier will come under even more scrutiny as emphasis on accountability increases among clients. The best way to build a long-term relationship is to be absolutely honest in all your dealings with clients. Courtesy is paramount. Policies of doing business must be put in place early in your relationship and followed consistently. Reputation and character are formed and judged by daily actions. It takes years to build a reputation, but only seconds to ruin it.

The line between the realms of farriers and veterinarians will be more closely monitored. State practice laws will be tested. Lawsuits will be brought against perceived violators. Liability insurance will be a necessity. Farriers will not only have to be wary of client legal action if something goes awry, but there will be increasing pressure from veterinarians with little formal training in foot care. This will be especially true from those veterinarians who see themselves as competing with farriers for business.

Veterinary education will continue to ignore the importance of the foot, due to a reduction in curriculum emphasis and faculty expertise in this area. New veterinary graduates will need to establish relationships with competent farriers in order to maintain successful practices dealing with performance athletes.

Clients will continue to value personality, integrity of appointments and follow-up service over craftsmanship *until* they are educated to recognize and value good work.

A - Athletics

Farriery is hard work and very stressful. Future farriers will recognize the need to treat their bodies like fine tools and properly maintain them. Exercise and working out will be seen as necessary to maintain longevity of business. Many farriers will choose to own and ride horses, which is a complementary exercise to the muscle stress of shoeing.

Directed and focused work is more efficient and easier on the body, therefore farriers seek ways to be more effective. They will pay more attention to their health, eating habits and nutritional supplements. Fitness will become a part of farrier training. More emphasis will be put on protecting the body from harmful effects of this hazardous work.

C - Craftsmanship

Future farriers will need to focus more on improving craftsmanship on the foot than in the shoes, due to the availability of every conceivable type of foot appliance. However, hand-eye coordination and confidence in skill application is best learned by doing forge work. Shoemaking helps a farrier understand feet. For this reason alone, forging is valuable even when machine-made shoes are available.

Once the shoemaking steps are learned and sufficient hammer control is mastered, effort is required to remain at a high skill level. All must pay the same price to attain the title of master craftsman. Time and patience, in addition to diligent attention to detail, are required. People who have not paid this price are unable to apply innovative solutions as well as those who have. Those who will pay the price to master their craft will be even better craftsmen than those we have today.

As with every profession, job satisfaction will be in direct proportion to the amount of craftsmanship a person puts into his or her work and the level of service he or she provides.

Shoeing competitions are valuable motivators to increase skill level. The discipline of preparation is what is most important. I hope competitions continue to be popular, for they may be, as now, the primary force in improving shoeing skill. The acceptance of class divisions has encouraged more participation and allowed interested craftsmen to move up through the levels. Competitions will be marketed to the public as "theater."

H - Horsemanship

Horsemanship skills are sorely needed today and will be even more rare in the future. Horse owners will probably be less able to train and handle horses than they are today. High-income horse owners will look to professionals to train and maintain horses that can be used for a few hours when they have small windows of time in an otherwise busy world.

While our understanding of horse behavior has increased in recent years, applying basic principles is lacking at most levels. A certain amount of "feel" or intuitive common sense is needed when working with a horse. This is the most difficult farrier skill to teach. The best way to gain it is by patiently working with and observing horses. There is no substitute for practical hands-on knowledge. I believe there will be greater opportunities in the future for farriers who have horse skills, since there will be fewer people who have paid the price to learn them.

Since people resist putting the time into learning the basics of good training, there will be more need for chemical restraint to allow safe shoeing work on less-than-fully-trained animals. Farrier-administered discipline may even be prohibited by law as well as unknowledgeable horse owners. Some farriers will leave the business because of this unrealistic expectation.

Farriers will need to position themselves as horse welfare advocates, teaching less experienced horse owners how to humanely care for their animals. Farriers need to distinguish between animal welfare and animal rights. The animal rights movement will become even more acceptable in the media and to a non-agrarian population. Farriers cannot endorse this position since the animal rights agenda advocates putting an end to horse domestication, horse training and horseshoeing.

E - Entrepreneurship

Most changes in farriery's future will come in the form of business management. Farriers will become computer savvy and learn to use contact management software that will keep track of clients and help manage their business. Effective businesses will have many long-term clients and few accounts receivable.

Successful farriers will develop systems to handle each part of the operation, spending more time working *on* their businesses as well as *in* them. There will be more multiple farrier practices, allowing for more time off and predictable schedules. The level of service will continue to increase as price and competition increases.

A very important part of service will be client education. This will mostly be provided one-on-one, but could also take the form of books, charts, specimens, videos or CDs. Many farriers will need training to become comfortable in a teaching environment. Top farriers will partner with highly regarded companies to promote the latest products that help keep horses sound or return them to soundness.

Owners will look to the farrier as a partner in their continuing education – not just someone with a strong back. Marketing will become a bigger part of the farrier business.

Relationship marketing will strengthen the client's confidence in knowledgeable farriers who understand horse behavior and physiology. Owners will look to the farrier as a partner in their continuing education – not just someone with a strong back. Marketing will become a bigger part of the farrier business. Value will be more important than price. The experience of having the farrier making a call will be valued as much as the service provided.

Competition will become keener since more people will long to get into an unregulated business without paying the price of a long apprenticeship or college degree. The expansion of products that remove various aspects of craftsmanship and physical work from the job will make this even more possible in the future.

Many farriers will market horse care products directly to horse owners from their mobile shops. This is one way they will develop other businesses early in their careers to supplement the farrier business, since it is so easy to literally get "kicked out" of it. A larger percentage of farriers will begin planning for retirement at the beginning instead of near the end of their shoeing careers.

R - Recreation

Farriers will be smarter about the use of their time in the future. Physical and mental relaxation will be a part of each day's activities. The value of a well-planned schedule will be a central focus of the farrier's day. Time for family and self will all need to be scheduled. Frequent vacations will break up the work schedule. Farriers will retire at a younger age than ever.

Farriers will place a greater emphasis on the professional nature of their work. Farriers will do the kinds of things professionals already do in other fields. These include continuing education, improved scheduling, reminders of appointments, keeping accurate records, hiring competent outside help, using innovative high-tech products and techniques, financial planning and presenting a professional image.

I believe the farrier business will be great in the future.

Six-Figure Shoeing

Chapter 4

How to Recognize and Strengthen Your Motivation

Chapter 4

How to Recognize and Strengthen Your Motivation

The Role of Motivation

Our motivation for doing anything is at the heart of our lives. What is important to you? Why is it important? What are the priorities in your life? Does how you spend your time align with what you say is important? How can you make your heart-felt desires and actions more congruent and enjoy all the blessings life has to offer? The answers to these questions and others come by examining your motivation.

Why did you choose to be a farrier? Are those reasons still valid? Farriery, like most careers, has its benefits and challenges. Being in business for yourself has its own set of problems.

Purpose and planning are significant parts of an emerging business. What is your purpose? Michael E. Gerber in his book *The E Myth* says, "Your primary aim is the vision necessary to bring your business to life and your life to the business. It provides you with purpose and energy." He also says, "The difference between great (successful) people and everyone else is that great people create their lives actively, while everyone else is created by their lives, passively waiting to see where life leads them next."

Most self-employed people follow a particular income curve with a new business. They start with it being a hobby or interest and allow it to progress into a job for a short time. Then they go through a period of high risk and high debt and, hopefully, high growth for a few years. Finally, the business matures and creates a steady income for a 10-to-20 year period. At that point, it may begin to decline for various reasons.

The objective is to physically generate a positive income stream as long as possible, then switch to a residual income stream that continues when you no longer do the business. This is especially important in the farrier craft, since, due to its highly physical nature, most people cannot keep it up forever. And working with horses, we can literally be kicked out of business!

Benefits

Here are seven benefits for choosing to be a self-employed farrier.

1. **You build your own dream by investing in your future.**

   There is only room for one person's dreams in any business. You either have direction or goals in your life, or you work for someone who does. You are free and responsible to create your own future. You can obtain as much as you are willing to pay the price to achieve.

2. **You are your own boss.**

   People who don't enjoy having someone looking over their shoulder and telling them what to do should be their own bosses. Creating a sustainable business requires tremendous self-discipline and focus. Freedom from suppression often stimulates creativity.

3. **You receive satisfaction and direct monetary rewards for hard work.**

   When professional service providers who work with their hands are paid for their knowledge and skill, the sense of completion they feel invigorates them. Setting goals and achieving them is fun. Your immediate monetary reward sustains the enthusiasm.

4. **You have a flexible work schedule.**

   You are able to select your own work hours. This freedom allows you to schedule the things you really want to do in your life. You can enjoy family time, vacation time and personal time, or you can put more time and effort into the business to make additional income.

5. **You interact with people and animals by serving them.**

   Having people depend on your service and skill gives meaning to your work and helps you feel needed and valued. In addition, animals are very accepting; being around them is good for a person's self-esteem.

6. **You interact with professional associates.**

   You work with people who have similar interests and share your love of horses. These include trainers, veterinarians, massage therapists, acupuncturists, chiropractors, dentists, grooms and other farriers.

7. **Your income potential is six figures.**

   If you provide superior service, master the skills of farriery and learn to manage your business effectively, you can achieve a six-figure income.

You will then be among the top 5% of farriers who have figured it out.

Challenges

While you experience great benefits being a farrier, you also face many challenges that accompany this business. Here are seven of them.

1. **Farrier work is hard physical work.**

   You must be physically strong and recognize you have a high risk of injury, even if you know what you are doing. Farriers must treat themselves as athletes.

2. **Most clients cannot tell the difference between good work and bad work.**

   You must educate your clients to recognize your work as better than that of the competition. Sell value over price through relationship marketing.

3. **There is no formal recognition as a profession.**

   There are no required exams or licenses. Anyone can claim he or she is a farrier, and many do.

4. **There is no formal system for learning the trade.**

   Schools differ greatly from one another and the curriculum is not standardized. Unless you have a coach or mentor, there is no one to look to for backup – it is all up to you.

5. **Extensive travel is required to specialize in a breed or type of horse.**

   The more specialized and skilled you become, generally, the more you have to travel.

6. **Self-motivation is required for skill improvement.**

   How fast you progress and get to new levels is entirely up to you. Competitions, clinics and working with a mentor provide the most help. Extra effort is required.

7. **Marketing and business positioning.**

   Though marketing and business positioning are not commonly taught, they have to be learned to establish and maintain a long-term business.

Balance

Enjoying balance is important in horseshoeing and in life. Horseshoeing has great income-producing potential. It can bring tremendous career satisfaction. But it is also very susceptible to producing practitioners who live completely out of balance. Some things are simply more important than others in our lives. Many farriers, including myself, have had to learn this truth through personal experience. Long-term effectiveness can only be achieved by organizing our lives around our personal priorities. Understanding our motivation helps us do this.

Principles of Motivation

The following eight principles can help you understand your motivation:

1. **Do what makes you feel good about yourself.**

   To feel good, you must *be* good. You must be good at what you do and do what is good. To *be* good, you must build your skill base. This means pushing yourself to study and practice. To *do* good, you must choose to be kind, considerate and grateful, always looking for opportunities to practice these virtues. Exercise self-discipline. Recognize that competency equals skill plus character.

2. **Be humble and teachable.**

   Recognize your level of knowledge and skill. Knowledge is being proud you know so much; wisdom is being humble that you know no more. Be open to increasing your understanding. Learn from everyone. Choose mentors. Seek out

growth experiences. Turn daily experiences into wisdom.

3. **Visualize with clarity.**

   Visualize where you want to be and what it would be like if you were already there. The clearer the mental picture, the stronger the motivation to achieve it. Imagine yourself at the skill level you want to be and having the kind of business you want. This adds to motivation.

4. **Expect success.**

   You get from life what you expect, so expect success. Self-suggestion is an important part of motivation. Self-suggestion involves planting an idea or desire in your mind. This can be done by repetition, by visualization or both. Write out your positive affirmations and review them several times each day. Soon you will be living them.

5. **Determine your purpose.**

   Purpose gives your actions meaning. Define what you value and ask why you do things. Write and internalize a mission statement for yourself and your business. Your purpose should dominate all you do. How you behave says a lot about who you are and what your purpose is. Here is mine:

   I guess you could say I'm the horse's best friend. I help those who shoe horses become horse-foot-care experts. As a 40-year farrier with a Ph.D., I know the horse's foot – both in theory and in fact. Along the way, I've developed a sequential learning system that transcends the traditional classroom experience. Using the educational materials I've developed from years of hands-on experience, my students tell me they learn more, learn faster, and do better. My learning systems help people master farrier skills, one step at a time, to help horses stay sound one foot at a time.

6. Seek growth experiences.

Growth comes from trying new things and looking at things differently, even from failure. Growth does not necessarily come from success. You have a limited time to be in business. As New York farrier Steve Kraus says, "There are only so many horses in your body." But there are no limits (except those set by yourself) in how much you can grow in that amount of time.

7. Be a self-starter.

Actions regulate feelings. By acting enthusiastically, you can become enthusiastic. Your greatest challenge when doing anything is to start. Once you begin, the power to complete comes. Goethe wrote, "Each indecision brings its own delay and days are lost lamenting over lost days. Are you in earnest? Seize this very minute! What you can do, or dream you can, begin it! Boldness has genius, power and magic in it. Only engage, and then the mind grows heated. Begin, and then the work will be completed."

8. Obey yourself.

You strengthen your character by making and keeping promises. You weaken it by not keeping promises to yourself and others. When you fail to do the things you expect of yourself, you lose self-respect and may lose the respect of others. Feelings of accomplishment and peace of mind come when you do what you say you will do. A key to obeying yourself, or having integrity, is to be realistic in saying what you will do. Do the little things before tackling the big ones.

Self-examination

Self-examination is necessary to determine your appropriate livelihood and your motivation for doing it. You must continually ask yourself the following questions about if you are doing what you really want to do, and if is it right for you. The answers provide the motivation for your continued growth and achievement. I have given some of my answers. Yours will be different.

1. How do you see farriery?

I see farriery as a craft requiring a mental and physical balance. It is physically demanding but exhilarating work that brings proportionate financial reward. Horseshoeing is spiritually stimulating because it connects us to Nature and one of God's noblest creatures, the horse. It is a career that, when mastered, has more income potential than many other traditional careers that deal directly with the care and welfare of horses. Farriers form a firm foundation for the greatest athlete in the world by sculpturing the hoof from a mess of deformity to a thing of beauty. Dr. Matthew Mackay-Smith of *Equus* magazine says, "Farriers are the highest paid sculptors in the world." We make it possible for individuals to soar to emotional and spiritual heights that are not possible without their association with the noble horse. We allow people to obtain a release from today's impersonal, inanimate society by connecting them to nature.

2. What must you learn to master the farrier's craft?

At first glance, it appears we must only learn to use tools to create an effectual unity of metal and hoof. As we gain experience and ask questions, we discover a need to learn about anatomy, physiology, biomechanics, kinetics, genetics, geometry, trigonometry, nutrition, growth, pathology, behavior modification, gait analysis and training, self-mastery, self-reliance, public relations, accounting, tax planning, organization and efficiency, in addition to blacksmithing, metallurgy and welding. We must continually learn from our experiences and add to our knowledge base. As we increase in knowledge and competent skill, our value to our clients increases.

3. What character virtues assure success?

All character virtues are needed, in some degree, to assure success. The Boy Scout law and the Cowboy Code (see Appendix 5 for a description of the Boy Scout law and the Cowboy Code) contain good summaries. Ben Franklin describes a process in his autobiography for incorporating character traits or virtues into one's life. He worked on it every day. Examples of important character virtues can be found in the world's best-selling book, the Holy Bible:

a. Skillful mechanic or craftsman (worker and artificer) such as Tubal-cain.

b. Faithfulness of a patriarch such as Abraham.

c. Sense of humor of a matriarch such as Sarah.

d. Persistence and patience of a suitor such as Isaac.

e. Patience and animal husbandry skills of a servant such as Job.

f. Self-sufficiency and persistence of a seaman such as Noah.

g. Loyalty and devotion of a daughter-in-law harvest worker such as Ruth.

h. Faith and fitness of a shepherd such as David.

i. Strength and determination of a warrior such as Samson.

j. Vision of a special mother such as Mary.

k. Dexterity and steadiness of a carpenter such as Joseph.

l. Charismatic leadership of a master teacher such as Jesus.

m. Firmness and concentration of a fisherman such as Peter.

n. Love and "people skills" of a disciple such as John.

o. Care giving of a physician such as Luke.

p. Rhetoric and eloquence of a lawyer (and tent maker) such as Paul.

4. What attitudes are essential for success?

Our attitudes reflect our priorities and view of the world. We can shift our existing attitudes to include the following ones.

a. Decision to be successful

The single most consistent ingredient among successful business people is making the decision to be successful. Set income goals and work hard to achieve them. The most successful farriers have been willing to pay the price to make their goals become a reality.

b. Tolerance for pain

Pain becomes insignificant (at least *less* significant) if your work has purpose and meaning. People who have earned achievements in any field recognize this. Dr. Jean-Louis Etienee, who walked alone to the North Pole, said, "There are two great times of happiness – when you're haunted by a dream, and when you realize it. Between the two there's a strong urge to let it all drop. But you have to follow your dreams to the end. There are abandoned bicycles in every garage because their owner's backsides got too sore the first time they rode them. They didn't understand that pain is a necessary part of learning." I would add that farrier tools can be found in everyone's tack room because people thought they could do horseshoeing with no coaching and no pain. All farriers who are motivated to become the best they can know better.

c. *Concern for horse's welfare*

Farriers who are motivated to provide great service, and are sincerely concerned about the overall welfare of the horses they shoe, have great value in the minds of their clients. When clients feel satisfied that their horses that mean so much to them are comfortable and well taken care of, your business as their service provider will last a lifetime. Express your concern often for their horse's welfare.

d. *Desire to learn more*

One of the most important attitudes is the desire to learn more. Michael E. Gerber states in *The E Myth*, "People who succeed in business don't do so because of what they know, but because of their insatiable need to know more. Conversely, the problem with failing businesses I've encountered is not that the owners don't know enough . . . but that they think they know enough. And so they spend their time defending what they know, rather than discovering what they don't."

e. *Persistence to make dreams realities*

In a study, researchers asked students, parents and teachers, "What is the most important factor contributing to success in life?" In Asian countries, the universal response was "hard work" – so students there work hard. By contrast, Americans replied, "intelligence." In other words, if you are intelligent, you shouldn't have to work hard. If you're not, there is no point in trying. I suggest you will be wiser and happier if you teach your children (and believe it yourself) that they can achieve success and satisfaction in any field by persistence and hard work. Both intelligence and diligence will make anyone's goals a reality.

5. What attracted you to horseshoeing?

Examine the major turning points in your life, those experiences in which you had a major paradigm shift or new way of seeing things. Ask yourself what you have had to learn to get where you are today. Here are a few of my turning points.

- My favorite toy was a hammer given to me for Christmas when I was two years old. I slept with it. As a child, I loved tools and making things.

- I adopted Gene Autry's Cowboy Code and tried to live by it. My heroes were the "good guy" movie and television cowboys.

- My first horse was a pony I received when I was seven. I loved horses, and felt connected to Nature as I learned to ride and work around them.

- I watched and admired horseshoers who came to our farm, especially Marshall "Buster" Conklin. He was also a cowboy and roper.

- A trip to Arizona at the age of 13 convinced me to become a real cowboy.

Lonnie Howard was my mentor and hero. He could shoe a horse as well as any farrier. He convinced me to go to college and learn welding and other useful skills.

- I did a research paper for my Freshman English Composition course titled, "The Art of Horseshoeing." I applied to the Cal Poly Horseshoeing School as a result of writing that paper. It took me two years to get in.

- While a senior at Cal Poly working with Ralph Hoover, I wrote a senior paper titled, "Horseshoeing Iron and Forge Work." Later, I published this as a booklet. Ralph Hoover gave me a chance to teach horseshoeing at Cal Poly, Montana State and Penn State. I found teaching accelerated my own learning.

- I liked the honesty, skill-building and lack of pretense that went with horseshoeing. The satisfaction of completing a job and getting paid for it motivated me. The self-reliance and monetary reward were especially appealing after working as a cowboy for low wages.

- My mother and my wife have both had a great influence on me. My mother was horse-crazy and a student of horse behavior and welfare. She organized the first 4-H Light Horse Club in the U.S. with 62 members. My sister became the president and I was one of the only two boys in the club. My mother raised and showed champion Welsh ponies for 40 years. I met my wife, a horse owner, as a result of a speech she gave on horseshoeing in college. We have enjoyed riding together on the trails of life for over 30 years.

6. **What do you need to do to progress?**

   a. *Aim to consistently create a profit through your business.*

   A farrier constantly striving to improve the difficult-to-master hand-eye coordination of forging and shoeing skills frequently neglects business and personal development. Frustrations arise from a lack of business training. Most farriers be-gin their farrier business part-time until they build up the clientele and stamina necessary to develop a full-time business that is profitable and rewarding. As Colorado farrier Jeff Rodriguez says, "Who cares if you can shoe a horse correctly, if you can't extract a reasonable living from the effort?" By examining, understanding and applying successful business principles, you will be able to consistently create a profit through your business.

   b. *Build a solid foundation by visualizing your success.*

   As farriers, we build the horse's foundation, similar to building a house. If we do not create a solid foundation, it doesn't matter how pretty the rest of the house is, eventually, the house will not be able to support itself and will fall. To ensure this doesn't occur, house builders use blueprints to visualize the finished house. When they follow the blueprint, they make the architect's dream a reality with precise detail.

   c. *Shift your mindset.*

   People see the world in different ways that influence

the way they think and act. To achieve the highest levels of success and achievement, shift your mindset from the status quo and look toward new vistas. In farriery, you can also follow maps and blueprints that can be followed to have a successful and rewarding career. And to reach the highest pinnacle, you have to make certain mind shifts – ones that come about as a result of turning points or key experiences in our lives. I have shared some of mine. Yours will be different. Ask yourself, "What mind shifts do I need to make to set up the foundation I want for my own success?"

7. Questions to shift minds

a. *Where are you?*

On what level is your skill and farrier business? Be honest with yourself. There is a difference between experience/education and expertise. Time alone doesn't form skill. Attendance alone at an educational clinic or in a class can't compare with the long-term value of focused coaching and one-on-one instruction from a qualified teacher. Skill is hammered out one blow at a time through diligent practice. A coach or mentor helps you maintain the focus you need to move from where you are to the next level. Still, all true education is self-education. Be aware of your ignorance. You have to commit to learning the elements of farriery for yourself. Don't be afraid to say you don't know when asked questions that surpass your present understanding. Instead, let your clients know your willingness to help by saying, "I'll find out and let you know." Position yourself as a problem solver. Commit to taking responsibility for horse/client welfare by helping clients learn to enjoy their horses even more.

b. *Where do you want to go?*

Achievement is accomplishing what you want in life. Success is a journey and reflects enjoyment of your achievements. Do you have a personal or business mission statement? Can you state what you want to accomplish in a few words? For example, mine is: *I provide sensible solutions for soundness by forging firm foundations*. Take some time to reflect on what you and your business are about. With a vision of what you want to accomplish, you can figure out the steps necessary to get you there. Set specific goals that can be measured. Strive for the best within yourself. Learn the fundamentals of the craft. Practice the process. Obtain credentials. Surveys show these are unimportant to customers, but earning them helps you develop patience, perseverance and self-confidence.

c. *How do you get there?*

Determine the most important aspects of your mission, then organize and execute around those priorities. Time management is really control of events, not control of time, so strive to control the events in your life. Money buys time and works *for* us, so strive to make your money only once. Plan to keep it, and make it work. This requires self-discipline and shifting your mind from the paradigm of making money you spend to making money that makes more money. Most people struggle with managing their lives, requiring some kind of external discipline imposed on them. Procrastination indicates lack of self-discipline. If you have trouble with procrastination, impose some discipline and set up a reward system for accomplishment. Learn to work efficiently by breaking down the elements of a job into a workable process. Master the elements of the process and you will master the job.

d. *Who will help you?*

Associate with leaders in the industry who can help you get where you want to be. Working with mentors, trainers and coaches can lead to making much more progress than you could on your own. Ask questions of your clients. Observe great horses and horsemen. Acquire a training library. Subscribe to industry publications. Learn every day. Be selective in what you apply; not all information is of equal value. If you struggle with what you should read, ask a mentor what would be most helpful. Study training materials prepared by those who are where you want to be.

e. *What questions do you need to ask?*

We learn by asking questions. Make notes. Study and internalize material. Practice techniques before trying them on a client's horse. Embark on a journey of self-discovery. This exercise will help you understand others.

f. *What do you need to do to help others get what they want?*

Noted motivational speaker Zig Ziglar says, "You can have anything in life you want, if you just help enough other people get what they want." Strive to make and keep customers. Find a need and uniquely fill it with your service. Obtain input from all parties involved to create the best solution.

g. *How do you stay on top and still make progress?*

Strive for balance at the level of practice you choose. Practice daily. Seek renewal. Strengthen your motivation by asking the foregoing questions. Continue to learn and keep growing. Plan ahead. Protect yourself. Hire good help when needed.

h. *How much will it cost to start your business?*

Part of building a foundation for business success is determining your equipment needs and start-up inventory. While initial schooling is important, how you manage your learning experiences after school is much more significant to your success.

Try to realistically estimate your investment. You can use a farrier supply catalog for this exercise. Ask yourself, how long will it take to recover this investment?

SCHOOLING COST

Transportation costs

School tuition

Room and board

Books and videos

Lost income while at school and building business

Advanced training after school – clinics, coaching, classes, conventions, etc.

TOTAL

BASIC HAND TOOLS COST

Safety boots

Leather apron

Safety glasses

Ear plugs

Hoof nippers

Hoof gauge and dividers

Hoof knife

Hoof rasp + handle

Driving hammer

Clinchers

Crease nail pullers

Clinching rasp + handle

Clinching block

Pull-offs

Hoof testers

Clinch cutter

Center punch

Marker or chalk

Rounding hammer

Clipping hammer

Fitting vise-grip pliers

Tongs, 4 pair - 1/4", 5/16", 3/8", 1/2"

Fuller

Nail stamp

Nail pritchel

Metal ruler

Tool box

TOTAL

MOBILE SHOP TOOLS COST

Pickup truck

Truck bed topper

Shoe, nail and pad racks

Tool storage

Anvil

Anvil stand

Vise

Forge and propane tank

Drill press

Grinder or sander

Welder(s)

Band or saber saw

Hand drill

Motorized burr

Shoe scale

Light and fan

Extension cord

TOTAL

HOME OFFICE COST

Office furniture

Computer and printer

Accounting and tax preparation software

Contact management software

Phone(s)

File and shelf storage space

TOTAL

i. *What are the operating costs of doing business?*

- Other start-up costs include marketing materials such as business cards, brochures or flyers, as well as ads, phone listing and gifts for new clients.

- You will also need to stock your mobile shop with inventory to perform your work, such as assorted keg shoes and bar stock, assorted nails, pads, hoof packing, hoof patching materials, forge fuel and assorted fasteners.

- You will have to provide your own insurance to cover health/accident, disability, liability and life insurance. Include the expenses of vacation, sick leave and retirement.

- Office expenses may include a secretary, accounting and tax preparation. Don't forget the cost of continuing education. Be sure to set aside money to pay taxes.

j. *What must you do to stay fit for this business?*

- Horseshoeing is physically demanding work requiring physical strength, manual dexterity, horsemanship, hand-eye coordination and mental concentration. The ability to earn a living, as well as the ability to learn marketable skills, will be severely limited if one is not fit for the work.

- Since we do not have an organized government-sponsored system for learning farriery in America, those who want to practice higher-level work must work harder than the average person. We must read and study, watch clinicians and practice techniques until they are a part of us. According to Dr. William Bennett's Cultural Literacy Report, 80% of Americans have not read a book in the last year. Fifty percent have not read one book since high school. You will be in the top 1% if you make it a habit to read and study regularly. Earl Nightingale said that an hour of study a day on a given topic or subject can make anyone a foremost expert in their field in five years. Ralph Waldo Emerson said that the difference between the person you are now and the person you will be next year is the books you read and the people you meet. Also add to the list the clinics you attend and the videos you watch.

k. *What are the biggest obstacles to a farrier's success?*

A national survey revealed poor business skills to be the biggest obstacle preventing farriers from achieving success. The most common errors were:

- Entering business with limited understanding of finance and the costs of doing business.

- Inability to establish a diverse network of contacts and a good referral base.

- Little or no long-term direction for business (inability to make it in off-season months due to lack of planning).

- Bad business management and poor tax planning.

l. *What problems cost farriers money?*

- Rising insurance and living costs without a corresponding increase in charges.

- Inefficiency at the anvil or under the horse.

- Badly behaved horses leading to injury.

- Not knowing how to take income tax deductions.

- Interest from business debt on new equipment and business or inventory.

- Inability to properly maintain inventory.

- Uncollected receivables.

m. *What are the rewards?*

If we compare the wants and needs of farriers, veterinarians and horse owners (contrasted with punishments to avoid), it might look like this:

Rewards Farriers Want to Gain	Punishments Farriers Want to Avoid
a. A good living	a. Wasting time or losing money
b. Recognition by peers	b. Being found out for practicing above level
c. Praise and admiration of clients	c. Lacking confidence or being insecure
d. Physical health	d. Getting hurt; being unhealthy
e. Time for fun	e. Having no time for fun

Rewards Veterinarians Want to Gain	Punishments Veterinarians Want to Avoid
a. A good living	a. Losing money
b. Recognition by peers	b. Being found to be unknowledgeable
c. Praise and admiration of clients	c. Feeling insecure about horse treatment
d. Advancement in their careers	d. Wasting time
e. Success in society	e. Being socially rejected

Rewards Horse Owners Want to Gain	Punishments Horse Owners Want to Avoid
a. Sound, comfortable, "happy" horse	a. Pain or death of horse
b. Relationships with professionals	b. Waiting for farrier or veterinarian
c. Horse maintenance without hassle	c. Horsekeeping becoming an extra effort
d. Pleasure from professional's visit	d. Disliking professional's visit
e. Cooperation with service people	e. Having conflicts with service people

Ultimately, a farrier must avoid doing anything that takes away the horse owners' ability to experience pleasure with their horse habit. Remember! People don't care how much you know until they know how much you care!

Levels of Motivation

What causes you to be motivated to master farriery? Do you desire to help horses and their owners achieve their potential? Do you gain satisfaction from using your creativity and problem-solving abilities to discover solutions?

An essential part of being successful is being involved in meaningful work. It doesn't matter why you decided to get into farriery; what matters is that it is meaningful to you in some way. That meaning might come from any of seven different motivations, which are hierarchical and may change throughout your career.

Which of these factors are most important and give you meaning in your work?

The first and lowest level of motivation is being **addicted to work**. Addiction causes you to avoid the reality of what is happening to you and those around you. Even though your work may bring you monetary reward and temporary satisfaction, it can lead to tremendous dissatisfaction because of the inevitable results of long-term life imbalance and neglect of important people in your life.

The second level of motivation is the **immediate monetary reward**. Money is used by some farriers as a way of "keeping score." It can become an end in and of itself, causing one to push beyond his or her physical limitations. People (clients and family) quickly sense if money is more important to you than they are.

The third level of motivation is the **personal freedom of being an independent worker**. This is a strong motivation for those who have experienced dependency on, and manipulation by, their bosses. Of course, you still depend on your client for payment, but you are independently responsible for the quality of work you turn out and the perception of its quality by the client.

The fourth level of motivation is the **challenge of completing a difficult task**. Working on difficult tasks that lead to personal growth motivates some people. They like to work in challenging environments and see their completed work. They enjoy the growth that results.

The fifth level of motivation is the **challenge of mastering all of the skills of farriery**. Farrier skills are varied, comprise many subjects, and require much attention to detail and effort to master. The challenge to master a field in which so few are willing to pay the price is an exciting opportunity and motivates some farriers.

The sixth level of motivation comes from **satisfying clients and feeling their dependence on your skill**. Wanting the client to be happy with your performance and to express a dependence on you as a horse health care provider can be a strong motivation.

The seventh and highest level of motivation is **to provide for the overall welfare of the horse**. Domesticated horses are not capable of providing for themselves or expressing appreciation. Knowing they are comfortable and well taken care of adds meaning and motivation. This kind of motivation will be achieved as you discover your purpose and continually strive to improve your skills.

Levels of Motivation

Level 1	Addicted to work
Level 2	Immediate monetary reward
Level 3	Personal freedom of being independent

Level 4	Challenge of completing a difficult task
Level 5	Challenge of mastering all farriery skills
Level 6	Satisfying clients and feeling their dependence on your skill
Level 7	Provide for the overall welfare of the horse

Continuous motivation comes from doing what you say you will do. When you fail to keep a commitment to improve yourself because of laziness or a lack of desire, you set yourself up for future failure. Your inability to follow through causes you to lose your confidence and self-respect. To feel consistently motivated, you must not only obey yourself but be realistic about *what* you want to achieve and *when* you want to achieve it.

Being realistic implies you must sequentially progress and work from one level to the next. Do not expect to be able to perform complex operations without first being able to master basic operations. If you are not realistic, you can't keep the commitments you have made to yourself and, as a result, you lose confidence and hope.

The most successful individuals in any career are those who do what gives them a sense of satisfaction. They feel good about themselves. If you are at peace with yourself and your situation, you will find it much easier to motivate yourself. Like Confucius said, "Choose the work you love, and you will never have to work a day in your life."

Frustration comes when we are not happy with our work or ourselves. We lose the vision of why we're doing our work. We either need to change our work or change ourselves.

To be motivated from within and achieve excellence each day, visualize your objectives clearly. You must not only know what you want to accomplish but you must "see" the steps in accomplishing it. Success not visualized is rarely achieved. So picture yourself achieving excellence in your mind long before you achieve excellence at the anvil or under the horse.

Character Traits

I have divided the character traits of those who desire to master the art of farriery into seven areas. Using the word MASTERY as an acronym, they are as follows: **Motivated, Achiever, Self-confident, Teachable, Excellent, Responsible,** and **Yearns**.

M - Motivated

To successfully master farriery, take time to understand what motivates you. This gives you the capacity to grow and improve. A good teacher can enhance the process for you, but if you always have to look to others for motivation, you will never achieve the highest realms of success.

Do you desire to help horses and their owners achieve their potential? Do you gain satisfaction from using your creativity and problem-solving abilities to discover solutions? Your motivation or desire, like a spark, may be very small at first. It is the commitment to act on that desire that fans the spark, causing it to burst into flame. A powerful motivation, a burning desire, will allow you to achieve excellence.

No one but you can determine your level of commitment. It takes discipline to continually follow through with your commitments, and it takes dedication to endure the challenges that follow once you make the decision. Your motivation to become a master of the craft must come from within. Your inner motivational flame has to be continuously fanned by discipline and dedication to achieve success.

A - Achiever

High-achieving farriers know that risk and failure are part of learning. They are committed to setting goals, and they have the vision to see them through to completion. Many people never decide to get started for fear of failure. As a result, they rarely achieve anything. As Goethe said,

"Seize this very minute! What you can do, or dream you can do, begin it! Boldness has genius, power and magic in it."

Achievement is a measurement of what you have accomplished. As you apply principles and improve in skill, you will progress from one level to the next. This progression, or movement, is what constitutes achievement.

Where you finish is more important than where you start. Your dreams become realities as you pay the price to progress through countless hours of self-discipline and focus.

Achievers are dedicated, persistent and diligent in finishing what they have started. Once they arrive at the goal they have set, they set new goals. As Denis Waitley said in *The New Dynamics of Winning*, "Success is a process that continues, not a status that you reach."

Never be satisfied with reaching a particular level of knowledge or skill. Be committed to a quest for excellence through lifelong learning. Realize you can never know all there is to know about your profession.

S - Self-confident

How well you do anything directly relates to your self-concept in that area. Individuals in any walk of life are only as effective as they believe themselves to be. Self-concept is either driven by self-limiting beliefs or self-liberating beliefs. For example, the four-minute mile was believed by many to be impossible to break. In 1954, Roger Bannister became the first man to run a mile in less than four minutes, with a time of 3 minutes, 59.4 seconds. One month later, his record was broken by John Landy in 3 minutes, 58.8 seconds. Two months later, Bannister tied Landy's record and beat him in a race. Today, many athletes consistently run the mile in under four minutes. Were individuals prior to Bannister's time incapable of running a four-minute mile? Yes, because they believed it couldn't be done. As a result, they couldn't run faster than their limiting beliefs. Once the mind barrier was broken, others successfully accomplished this feat.

This same principle applies to horseshoeing. If you are sure you can't shoe a horse in less than two hours for a certification exam because you have never done it, you will not be able to do it during the examination. If you break down each part and work on improving your efficiency and speed in each part, you can and will do it.

In 1986, I competed in Closeburn, Scotland, on the North American Horseshoeing Team. One of the competitions was to make a rocker-bar shoe and a draft shoe, and shoe one foot on a Cly-desdale horse in 70 minutes. At first, I felt this was impossible. As I practiced at home, my belief that I could complete the contest within the time limit was strengthened. My confidence grew. In the first round at the actual competition, I burned up two of the rocker-bar shoes in the massive coke fire as I was striking for Dave Duckett. My confidence plummeted. With 35 minutes to go, Dave decided the calked Clydesdale shoe we had made was too long. He told me to go to the other shop and cut another piece of stock. We still finished within the time limit. He had practiced consistently and was so confident of his skill, he knew he was capable of completing the work even with the time restraint.

Later, during the last round with Duckett as my striker, I finished the run within the time limit, doing the best job I could do at the time because I had paid the price in practice.

The key is to practice competing with yourself in your everyday work and at dedicated practice times. Practice like you're competing and compete like you're practicing. Your beliefs about what you can or can't do are shaped during practice. When you know what you are capable of, and you work toward the highest standard, you will develop the confidence to do well in competitions or examinations.

Here are five things you can implement immediately to improve your self-concept.

1. Convert self-limiting beliefs into self-liberating beliefs through diligent and focused practice.

2. Learn what you are capable of compared to a high ideal or standard, and constantly seek to improve your work to match that standard.

3. Develop positive mini-self concepts in all areas of your work. Master the seven skill areas at whatever level you are on. Balance your business so your overall self-concept is positive and your relationships are fulfilling.

4. Break out of comfort zones by challenging yourself on a daily basis. Do things that are hard to do. Eliminate "justification" from your vocabulary and thinking. Accept responsibility for your skill level and begin mastering the skills you need to move up to the next level.

5. Establish a clear vision of what you want to be and live your life congruently with that vision. Maintain a high self-esteem by doing

things that allow you to feel valuable and worthwhile. Conversely, don't do things that cause you to doubt your worth. Improve your competence in all areas and strive to be the best at what you do.

When you work to achieve competence, you simultaneously improve the power of your mind, your self-confidence and the quality of your work. As the quality of your work improves, your self-esteem improves, and you feel more and more valuable to the clients you serve. Then, you will feel comfortable selling your value to your clients.

It takes emotional endurance and mental toughness to keep climbing the never-ending road to success even in the face of defeat or disappointment. Each of us struggles when a horse dies after we have worked diligently to save it from a devastating illness. It takes mental toughness to "keep on keeping on" when things get tough in business and in life. But if you are patient and have a good support group, you can enjoy success in your life.

T - Teachable

You must remain teachable to learn and progress. This means remaining open-minded and implementing the recommendations of those who have gone before you. These people are called mentors. They can help you get from where you are to where you want to be in the shortest amount of time with the least amount of trial and error.

Teachable farriers have a thirst for knowledge and can acquire good judgment and wisdom from their experiences. They are coachable. A coach or mentor acts as a filter of experience to sort out information and present it in effective way so you can apply it.

All lessons of life must be repeated until they are learned. This is true in horseshoeing and in life. Denis Waitley, coach to Olympians, has said, "A lesson will be presented to you in various forms until you have learned it. When you have learned it, you can then go on to the next lesson."

E - Excellent

Strive for excellence in all areas of your business and life. Do what you say you will do. Honesty and integrity are essential values in developing rapport and trust with people.

Be creative and innovative. Mediocre farriers master technique and become slaves to it. The very best farriers master technique, then transcend or move beyond it. Always look for a better way, but master the basics first.

Be willing to practice all of the skills of farriery to perfection.

Each of us has more to learn about farriery. Because it takes a lifetime to master this skill, be patient with your progress.

Compete against yourself, not others. Waitley also said, "Though we all tend to compare ourselves against others, the happiest people in life know they don't really compete against others. Their success comes from doing their best, based on their unique skills and goals. Instead of achieving or performing to impress the world or your peers, seek to do something that you love that is excellent and beneficial. You need no one else to measure you or your skill. Your audience is your own self-respect. Set your own internal standards for success."

Skill can only be properly defined and measured when there is a standard to strive for and be measured by. A standard is something that doesn't change. The word "perfection" in the Greek language means "progress toward completeness." Some have a tendency to make up the standard after they have made the error. We can choose to come up to the standard or make excuses. But the standard doesn't change.

In evaluating standards of skill mastery, consider these three principles.

1. An assessment of skill should measure the ability to meet a defined stan-

dard with a degree of accuracy and speed. The assessment itself measures the ability to perform the work. A time limit in a skill evaluation measures how accurately and efficiently a skill can be performed at that standard. Ability can be measured without a time limit; skill cannot.

2. A standard should be something that is defined in a clear and concise manner. The specific parameters of the standard to achieve a high level of skill must be written down and accessible to all. This way, an examiner can measure an individual at a well-defined and written standard, not what the examiner feels is his or her own standard or comparative ability to perform a task. This allows both the examiner and the examinee to measure the work performed against a specific "mark on the wall."

3. Meeting a standard does not happen by accident. Proper focus and discipline will allow anyone with commitment who takes personal responsi-

bility to achieve the standard and master a skill.

R - Responsible

No one else but you can take responsibility for your personal growth and development. Dependence on the approval of others strengthens weaknesses and keeps you from growing. Be accountable for your decisions and actions. An independent person will be better able to work with other professionals in an interdependent relationship to arrive at the best solution. A responsible person will never try to shift the responsibility for themselves to others.

Y - Yearns

Continually learn and share your love of farriery with enthusiasm. After you master a skill, you not only desire to teach others, you also yearn to know more and reach for a higher standard. Wisdom is the correct application of knowledge and experiences. It involves knowing what to do and when to do it. Your skill and experience help you arrive at a particular conclusion. Now, you must have the courage to act on your conclusions. Be willing to defend your action on the basis of principles.

Teach your clients the value of sensible solutions. If an owner suggests a popular or faddish technique or product you know violates time-tested principles, find the courage to explain why it isn't practical or sensible. Then use your skill and experience to sell and apply what you believe will work, based on your experience and common sense.

One of the reasons for doing this is that the teacher always learns more than the student, therefore the teacher should be the most interested student in the class.

Summary

Motivated self-starter with passion for work. Possesses enthusiasm for helping others.

Achiever who sets goals and takes risks. Displays dedication and persistence.

Self-confident and reliable service provider. Helps people enjoy their horses.

Teachable and coachable. Learns from own experience and selected mentors.

Excellent commitment and integrity. Increases personal standards and practices to perfection.

Responsible for decisions and actions. Takes care of self, business and dependents.

Yearns to learn and share. Commits to continuing education and practical application.

Chapter 5

How to Identify and Advance Your Business Level

Chapter 5

How to Identify and Advance Your Business Level

Improving Your Skill

I have observed that farrier businesses go through a sequential development. Sometimes business owners compress steps for various reasons, but rarely can steps be omitted. Each farrier pays a price for success.

To advance your business level, think about both short-term and long-term results you want. Each day, ask yourself how you can improve your efficiency and skill. And, periodically, review your business plan to stay focused and on-track.

Business levels are often not determined by skill levels. A different set of skills is necessary to build a successful business than are needed to build a precision horseshoe. By understanding where you fit on the career ladder, you will be able to understand the major emphasis and time needed to achieve the level of success you desire.

In this chapter, I have created a chart of the farrier business levels on the basis of credentials, knowledge and skill possession, market positioning and gross income. The income numbers in a level are arbitrary; they should be considered the median of a range that varies according to location, market types and individual initiative.

I have listed the American Farrier's Association (AFA) certification exam names as credentials in the various business levels. These are not an exact fit, but they have time limits, which are essential in determining skill (since skill is defined as accuracy plus speed).

As you will see, the British Worshipful Company of Farriers (WCF) equivalent skill levels are given in parenthesis. I have taken all of the farrier exams and believe that the British exams are a more accurate assessment of the higher skill levels than the American exams.

Farrier Career Business Levels
Based on Positioning and Income

Level	Title Credentials	Positioning Priorities	Average Years in Level	Average Gross Income
1	**Student/Apprentice** Capable helper Part time Works with supervision AFA intern (Apprentice)	Self-motivated-keen to learn *Commitment consciousness/confidence* Horsemanship study Become finishing expert	2 – 4	–
2	**Beginning Farrier** Safe worker Full or part time Works independently AFA certified (Journeyman)	Careful, dependable horseshoer *Safety consciousness/confidence* Anatomy study Become foot balance and cold shoe fitting expert	5 – 10	$25,000
3	**Working Farrier** Efficient craftsman Full time May use helper AFA journeyman (DWCF)	Skilled farrier *Client consciousness/confidence* Foot disease study Become shoe and clip fitting expert	10 – 20	$50,000
4	**Advanced Professional** Problem-solving artist/designer Knows anatomy/physiology Partners with veterinarians AFA therapeutic endors. (AWCF)	Therapeutic specialist *Professional/client liason consciousness/confidence* Communication study Become barshoe fitting expert	10 – 20	$75,000
5	**Respected Mentor** Accomplished farrier Mentor/trainer Clinic/seminar presenter AFA educator endors. (FWCF)	Experienced communicator *Student consciousness/confidence* Business study Become presentation expert	5 – 10	$100,000
6	**Recognized Leader** Accomplished farrier Employer/master Establish business systems Recognized in farrier trade	Effective systems *Employee consciousness/confidence* Horse industry study Become service expert	10 – 20	$125,000
7	**Established Celebrity** Accomplished farrier Has residual income Sells services <u>and</u> products Recognized in horse industry	Product sales volume *Consumer consciousness/confidence* Finance study Become marketing expert	10 – 20+	$150,000+

© 2001 Doug Butler Enterprises, Inc.

Chapter 6

How to Identify and Advance Your Skill Level

Chapter 6

How to Identify and Advance Your Skill Level

Analyzing Your Career

An individual farrier *is* his or her business, so if you want to improve your business, you must improve yourself. Work *on* your business until it works *for* you. Assess where you are, choose where you want to go and commit to the process of getting there.

Career analysis is really self-analysis. For most farriers, career analysis has been a mystery until now. One of the most difficult tasks for farriers is accurately discovering where they are in their career development. The foundation of learning is the admission of ignorance.

Over the course of several decades, I have successfully coached many farriers to high levels of skill and income. They had to admit where they were before they could progress. The level matrix with defined standards can help you turn mystery into mastery.

The skill levels in the following matrix are chosen on the basis of mastery of a particular skill. Mastery means you are no longer struggling with it – you can do it, you understand it and you can explain it to others.

One way to know your skill level is to ask yourself if you would feel comfortable being tested in these various areas at the sequential levels. The subject areas you should be confident in discussing and applying for each level are outlined in Appendix 3 with sample questions.

Farrier Career Business Levels Based on Balanced Skill

Skill Area	Student/Apprentice Farrier	Beginning Farrier
Foot Skill	Pull shoes. Clean out the foot. Clinch and finish accurately. Know shoeing sequence.	Trim and dress hoof safely and accurately. Nail safely and securely.
Anatomy Skill	Know common names and position of bones below the horse's knee; know names and functions of horny structures of foot.	Know scientific names of bones below knee; know names and functions of sensitive and elastic structures of foot.
Respect the Horse	Know how to hold and restrain a horse (head restraints) and proper working positions; know leg unsoundnesses.	Know how to train a horse for shoeing (leg restraints). Know horse conformations and consequences.
Respect the Client	Protocol with public. Perception of farrier. Presentation of self.	Protocol with client. Perception of business person. Presentation of self.
Iron and Forge Work	Recognize shoe types/sizes and nail types/sizes. Learn oxy and arc welding. Fit pads. Basic tool maintenance.	Fit keg shoes accurately and make keg shoe alterations with forge and welders. Advanced tool maintenance.
Economic Business	Understand costs of setting up and doing business. Maintain accurate records.	Know how to establish prices for farrier services; use telephone effectively; market services effectively.
Responsibility for Health	Strengthen leg and back muscles. Body position comfortable and safe.	Strengthen upper body. Develop physical stamina.
Summary/Comparisons	Student/Apprentice capable of helping a working farrier; learning to be efficient with tools. Work with supervision. *Chance of error is great.*	Beginning farrier capable of safely trimming, fitting and driving nails. Work completed independently. *Chance of error is reduced.*

Farrier Career Business Levels
Based on Balanced Skill (continued)

Skill Area	Working Farrier	Advanced Professional Farrier
Foot Skill	Trim foot for hot fitting. Nail consistently in sound horn in a line parallel to coronary band.	Accurately trim and dress the distorted foot of diseased horse.
Anatomy Skill	Know normal foot and leg structure and function, blood pumping mechanism of foot, tendons and ligaments of foot and leg.	Know blood circulation and nervation of leg. Know tendons and ligaments of limb and functions in movement.
Respect the Horse	Know and understand horse behavior and physiology. Know horse's gaits and defects.	Know horse foot pathology. Know how to read radiographs. Know biomechanics.
Respect the Client	Protocol with other farriers. Perception of associations. Presentation of profession.	Protocol with veterinarians. Know medical vocabulary to increase understanding and communication.
Iron and Forge Work	Make fullered shoes and fire weld; fit hand-made clipped and bar shoes accurately to the foot. Make tools.	Make and accurately apply therapeutic shoes using various processes. Design shoes and tools.
Economic Business	Calculate expense and profit per horse. Tax calculation. Business plan. Retirement plan.	Inventory control. Tax planning. Budgeting.
Responsibility for Health	Work on life balance. Develop physical endurance.	Develop patience. Strengthen emotional endurance.
Summary/Comparisons	Working farrier capable of efficiently making accurate shoes within a specified time period. Work to a standard. *Chance of error is minimal.*	Advanced professional capable of working with others to solve lameness problems. Work together. *Chance of error is shared.*

Chapter 7

How to Use a Business Plan to Help You Succeed

Chapter 7

How to Use a Business Plan to Help You Succeed

Farriery Is A Business

Like most modern businesses, farriery is moving from being technically driven to being management and business driven. Farriers must be good business people as well as expert technicians in order to operate a sustainable business. An important way to evaluate your start-up costs and see the big picture of how your business will grow is to develop a business plan. As Napoleon said, "For everything, you must have a plan."

A business plan is a planned approach of your vision and your best estimate of how you develop your business. A written business plan is used to construct the business, then keep it on track after it is in operation.

Having a farrier business plan makes obtaining money for start-up much easier. It demonstrates that you have done your home-

> *Having a farrier business plan makes obtaining money for start-up much easier. It demonstrates that you have done your homework and are prepared to run a sustainable business.*

work and are prepared to run a sustainable business. This is especially important if you need to borrow money for expansion as well as start-up. For example, a farrier may want to build a shop for shoe forging and/or to have clients come for professional services, but needs to finance it. Lending institutions or venture capital investors can look at the business plan and determine the feasibility of building the shop, projecting if it can be a profitable venture. Financial records showing previous years' income may also be included as part of the business plan.

Studies by Ohio State University show 70% of businesses succeed when they have a written, comprehensive business plan, while only 10% of businesses that do not have a written plan succeed. A business plan clearly helps one determine if the proposed business is feasible before any investment is made.

A business plan can be organized in a number of ways. These eight items should be included in your business plan.

1. Executive Summary

2. Business Organization

3. Marketing Plan

4. Financial Plan

5. Product Sales

6. Operations and Systems

7. Growth Plan

8. Appendix

1. Executive Summary

The Executive Summary compresses the entire business plan into one concise section. This briefly details your present situation and the specific objectives you have for your business. It takes into account shifts that may occur in the marketplace and how your business will respond to those changes. In addition, your Executive Summary should detail why you (and any business partners you might have) are capable of fulfilling the business objectives you have outlined.

The Executive Summary includes an outline of what you have learned from researching what horse owners want and need in your area. This could be your own research or data gathered through independent resource. Are you aware of trends in your business area? Are you aware of new products or findings that your clients may desire for their horses? Can you give educated opinions why these would be good, or not good, for their individual horses?

A description of the services you offer and the position you occupy among the competition is another part of this summary. Your prices for services should be well defined. This can be in the form of a cost sheet you hand out to clients, or something you use when writing bills or doing your business planning.

Include a mission statement that tells you why you decided to go into the farrier business and what you intend to achieve in it. This would clearly reflect your aspirations and how you plan to make them realities. Also write down your values so you can refer back to them often and determine if your business is on course. For example, if your dominant aspiration is to make a six-figure income from shoeing horses but this violates your value of spending a lot of time with family, in the long run you will find your satisfaction will not match up with your income.

Finally, compose a one-sentence statement or slogan, preferably an alliteration (words with the same initial letter or sound) that says what your company does. This can be used on your business card and in your advertising, too.

2. Business Organization

This section identifies how your business is organized. You can set up your business entity in several ways. (See Chapter 8.) Most beginning farriers start as a sole proprietorship. Later, forming a corporation may make more sense. You may need help from a professional advisor to determine which is best for you based on your personal situation and where you see your business in the future.

If you have others working for you, this is a good place to list the job responsibilities of everyone on your team. This helps clarify the roles and boundaries of those with whom you work. It also allows you to focus on what you do best.

3. Marketing Plan

A marketing plan is probably the most important section of your business plan, next to your financial statements. This shows how you will acquire new clients and keep the ones you already have.

The **first** section of your marketing plan should outline your company's purpose in more detail than the Executive Summary. Identify why you went into business and your success in business in the past, if applicable. Then identify your goals for the current year and for five years from now, plus the action plans needed to make them happen. Lay out your values, vision and mission statement here, again, since they drive your marketing efforts. Identify all products or services that you offer, and what the benefit of each is to the buyer. Identify your unique selling point or position (USP), which defines what sets you apart from others who offer similar farrier products or services. Ideally, this is in the form of a slogan or short commercial. The USP answers the question, why should a prospective client choose my services over those of the competition?

The **second** portion of the marketing plan summarizes the farrier industry, where it is now and where it is heading. Accurate reports on how much others are charging for their services and other business research in the industry can be found in the Farrier Supplies and Services segment of the *American Farriers Journal*, published in November of each year. Find out what issues affect the farrier industry the most in your area and determine how you plan to address them in your business.

Third, your marketing plan should include a S.W.O.T. This analyzes the Strengths, Weaknesses, Opportunities and Threats affecting your company. By completing this exercise, you can clearly identify in what areas of your business you need to spend more time, and what areas need less managerial concern. (See Chapter 10.)

Fourth, identify your target market. Who will want to buy your skill and expertise as a farrier? Why do customers buy from you? If you don't know that already, find out. You can do this in the form of a survey or just by directly asking them, "Why do you use me to provide farrier service for your horse(s)?" Surveying your customers at least once a year will allow you to know what your customers are thinking and identifying what things are important to them. In the process, you may become aware of other markets you could get into and other growth opportunities that exists.

Fifth, identify the main competitors in your geographic territory and in what areas of your business they compete. Don't underestimate your competition. Watching your competitors is just as important as listening to your customers. If you plan to provide exceptional service to your customers and stay ahead of others competing for the same business, you need to know what they are doing.

Sixth, detail your pricing strategy. Identify what each product or service will cost your clients and why. This helps you under-stand and value your services from the perspective of your client. For example, if a pair of horseshoes costs $5.00 to purchase and you charge the client $10.00, identify and write down why you have increased the price. Reasons might include the following: having money tied up in shoes, expense to carry them around, and the time and money to go to the farrier supply store or have them shipped to your business. (See Chapter 13.)

Seventh, determine how big your service area will be. Many things go into this decision, including the type of horses you shoe, use of time and travel charges. Some farriers find plenty to do in a 15-mile radius from home while others drive into several states. Deciding how big a territory you want is essential; it gives you a way to decide whether to accept new business yourself or refer it to another farrier.

Eighth, determine how much income you want to make each year, then figure out how you will achieve that goal given the market potential and resources you have available.

Ninth. Once you have a sales goal for the year, write down the marketing strategies and tactics you will use to make your goals a reality. Your marketing strategies indicate how you will position your business; your marketing tactics detail how you will make this positioning a reality.

The **tenth** part of your marketing plan includes a way to implement it. From the summary of your competitive advantage, write a clear positioning statement. A positioning statement summarizes how you differ from other farriers, what you specialize in, and why clients would want to come to you instead of someone else.

Eleventh, you will need a system to evaluate how your business is progressing, ensuring you are on track month-to-month or quarter-to-quarter. (Quarterly may be best as this is approximately when tax payments for sole proprietors are sent in.) This system evaluates how effective your marketing strategies have been in creating profit. You can calculate your profit level by doing a break-even analysis and a target profit analysis based on each strategy that you used to reach your goal. From this information, you can determine your return on investment (ROI). It should be much more than a normal balance in a bank savings account!

4. Financial Plan

This tells how money will flow through your business. A monthly budget will show when expenses and income are expected to be highest and lowest. A five-year expansion of this, showing the summary for years two through five, is useful to anticipate trends. Cash flow projections help anticipate capital and growth needs.

You will need a profit and loss statement or pro forma balance sheet for investors to review as well as for calculating taxes. Also, you will need a list of your assets and liabilities. Assets are what you own and liabilities are what you owe.

A break-even analysis shows how much it costs to offer your product or service for sale and is necessary to allow you to calculate profit.

Finally, you need a statement of how you intend to obtain funds and distribute profits.

Section 183 of IRS (Internal Revenue Service) Tax Code provides that a taxpayer cannot deduct expenses of an activity that are greater than income from that activity, if the activity is not engaged in for profit. Horse operations have been targeted where expenses are deducted for business when, really, the activity is a hobby. If you intend to deduct your horse-related expenses from your income taxes, you must consistently show a profit and justify those expenses.

Here are things the IRS uses to test if your horse operation is for profit.

A. Operated in a businesslike manner

1. Maintained good books (records) – cash or accrual accounting

2. Advertised in trade publications by name

3. Advertised by competing with or showing horses.

4. Relied on a professional showman and other experts

5. Attempted to diversity to prevent losses

6. Changed operation to increase profitability

7. Had a business plan or "prospectus"

B. Operation shows a profit two out of seven years

C. Time, effort and competent help are expended in carrying out the activity – Not recreational involvement only

D. Success in other similar ventures

E. Amount of profit is proportional to investment and assets

F. Facility design is utilitarian – Not for entertainment only

G. Horses are a capital asset – they can be depreciated

over three to seven years according to use

H. Use approved accounting procedures

1. Cash

a. All income included in year received

b. All expenses deducted in year paid

2. Accrual

a. Allows capitalization of breeding and training costs

- "Capitalized" means added to the cost of the horse. Syndicates deduct expenses only when materials are consumed, not when bills are paid.

b. Expenses are not recovered until the horse is put to use or sold

c. Larger corporations (receipts over $1 million) are required to use this system

5. Product Sales

In this section, you describe what products you will sell (for example, horseshoes), how you will obtain them and the percentage of mark-up they will have.

You may want to sell horse care or farm products to your clients. Some possibilities include feed supplements, hoof antiseptics or dressings, hoof tools, leg boots, farrier supplies and educational materials. Perhaps you could develop your own brand of products to sell to clients.

6. Operations and Systems

A major factor in the success of any business is operating systems. The more systematic you can make your business, the easier it will be. You need a pattern for doing things that can be well understood by your help. (See Chapter 8.)

An important part of any system is client contact and development. This includes relationship building by using database mailings, reminders and thank you notes, timely articles and information, gifts or audio tapes or booklets, newsletters and annual appreciation events such as picnics or seminars. Consistent contact with your best customers will help generate referral business. Ask for testimonial letters and take photographs of difficult cases to display to clients in a notebook portfolio kept in your truck.

It's important to use a contact management system to keep track of your clients as well as a bookkeeping system that is easy to learn and maintain. There are many computer programs that can be adapted to your business with a little customizing. We prefer *Access* and *Act!* for contact management and *Quick Books* for bookkeeping. Some computer programs like *Farrier Basic* and *Clincher* are designed specifically for farriers. Or you can use a card file or notebook system like *Farrier Forms*. When needed, hire professionals who understand your record-keeping systems.

Include how you intend to receive calls, schedule work, maintain inventory, invoice, and make and receive payments.

Also think about possible risks or threats to your business and develop a plan of action to meet them. How would you handle disability or sickness, liability problems, loss of a partner, unexpected competition or change in the marketplace?

7. Growth Plan

Here is the place to dream about what you could do with your business eventually. Pose questions about the future. How big do you want your business to grow? How big do you have to be to justify having employees or partnerships? How much do you want to make? How much debt are you comfortable with? How long do you want to stay in business? How will you exit and/or transfer your business?

8. Appendix

An appendix includes detailed resumes of all personnel, testimonial letters from satisfied customers, copies of promotional materials, including feature articles, contacts and agreements, and systems forms.

Summary

A business plan is very helpful when starting your business; it's essential if you are seeking capital investment. It also serves as a guide to keep the goals of your business central to your concern. Your plan can be modified and improved as the business changes. Such a plan will make your goals readily visible and help you stay on track.

Chapter 8

How to Use Systems to Run Your Business

Chapter 8

How to Use Systems to Run Your Business

Build Systems Into Your Business

Michael E. Gerber's book, *The E Myth Revisited*, has sold over 500,000 copies. He has helped re-engineer more than 15,000 small businesses to aid people in gaining control over and results from their businesses. His message is all about the importance of creating business systems or franchise models. This chapter discusses how farriers can apply Gerber's principles to their horseshoeing operations.

Businesses built with a franchise prototype (a system that is reproducible by ordinary people) have a success rate of 95%, compared to a 50% failure rate of new business start-ups (even those started by "brilliant" people). The Secretary of State of Colorado has stated that four out of five businesses are likely to fail in the first three years of operation.

Gerber says that at least 40% of businesses fail in the first year

and nearly 80% of those fail within five years, while 75% of franchise-type businesses succeed. The franchise system runs the business, and the people run the system. Your business has real integrity when you deliver what you say you will, exactly when you say you will do it. And systems help achieve that.

The basic, underlying belief of a franchise-type business is that the actual product or service of business is not *what* it sells, but *how* it sells it. The experience of buying the product is as important as the product itself. In fact, the true product of the business is the business itself.

The book, *The Experience Economy*, by Joseph Pine and James Gilmore, discusses this concept in detail. The authors maintain tailoring a product or service for each customer makes it impossible for competitors to replace you. This is the way to keep customers long-term. That's why it's important to ask yourself what you want your cus-

> *In fact, the true product of the business is the business itself.*

tomers to consistently experience from your business. Customer surveys are an effective way of doing this.

A Way of Doing Things

A system is defined as a set of things, actions, ideas and information that interact with each other, and in so doing, alter other systems. In business, a system is "a way of doing things" to produce a marketing result.

The system is the solution, or game plan, to get the results you want. The idea is to design a system that meets the customer's expectations better than any other. Make the *idea* behind the work of delivering product and service greater than the work itself. Sometimes the solution system requires high-tech software; other times just a simple checklist.

A great system is one that leverages or magnifies people to the point at which they can produce extraordinary results consistently again and again. In a successful system, every possible problem has been thought through. Each part is organized and every process defined in detail. The objective is to give

the customer consistent value beyond his/her expectations. Value is in the details.

The question that must constantly be asked is this: how can I create a business that is systems-dependent rather than people-dependent? How can I create an expert *system* rather than hire an expert? Great businesses are built by ordinary people doing extraordinary things. It is impossible to produce a consistent result in a business that has to depend on extraordinary people.

Order is the basis of systems. Most people crave order in this chaotic world. A business that looks orderly says you know what you are doing, that your business works, and that you can be trusted to deliver the expected results. Order is best created by following a detailed checklist or operations manual.

Refining operations to improve how systems work by constantly working *on* your business makes a truly successful enterprise. To do this, you must come to understand that your business is not your life. It is apart from you, with its own rules and purposes as it aims to find and

The primary function of your business is to serve your life, not consume it. Your goal is to make the business work predictably, effortlessly and profitably each and every day.

keep customers. The primary function of your business is to serve your life, not consume it. Your goal is to make the business work predictably, effortlessly and profitably each and every day. It must also work without you to free you for a fuller life.

One of the best explanations of a simple system for horseshoeing appeared in an article called "Run Your Business – Don't Let It Run You" written by Martin Kenny in the December, 1991, *American Farriers Journal*. His system is not for everyone, but it has proven to be a well-thought-out, organized way to run a business. Kenny schedules types of days with fixed intervals. He completes all of his work in daylight during a 44-hour week. It works for him in his practice area.

Change Ourselves First

Most of us would benefit from making our businesses more effective. But, in order for them to thrive, *we* must change. First, we have to change our idea of what a business really is and how to make one work so it can give us what we want.

The prevailing idea (called the Fatal Assumption by Gerber) is that if we are good at the technical aspects of our business, we understand a business that does a particular kind of work. The tragedy is that when we fall prey to the Fatal Assumption, the business that was supposed to free us from the limitations of working for someone else actually enslaves us. Suddenly, the job we could do so well becomes that job PLUS a dozen others we don't know how to do. And then, our entrepreneurial dream of our own business turns into a technician's nightmare.

The successful business has a good mix between the Entrepreneur, the Manager and the Technician. The Entrepreneur is the visionary, or dreamer, in us that lives in the future. The Manager is the practical part of us that craves order and lives in the past. The Technician is the doer who gets things done and lives in the present. These often conflict. An equally balanced mix would be ideal and would belong to an incredibly competent individual. However, typically, the Entrepreneur is 10%, the Manager 20%, and the Technician 70%. Each business tends to mirror its owner's personal lopsidedness.

Stages of Businesses

Businesses, like people, are supposed to grow and change. Businesses, if they survive, go through three phases of growth: Infancy, Adolescence and Maturity.

A business in infancy is one in which the business and owner are one and the same. You are the business. Then it changes. There is more work to do than you can get done. You work harder and longer, but with less enthusiasm. Then, you realize it won't ever all get done. You realize you don't own a business; instead, you have a highly stressful job.

Adolescence begins at the point in your business when you decide to get some help. Soon, you learn that no one is willing to work as hard as you do. No one has your ability, your judgment, your desire or your interest. You try to stretch your limits by doing more and eventually leaving your comfort zone. You feel despair and cynicism. Customers become a problem rather than an opportunity, and eventually you dissolve the business. Or, you can prepare for and embrace growth. Businesses that become small again die. Instead, you start over to build a business that will work because of your system, not because of you.

Maturity is the third stage of growth exemplified by the best businesses in the world. These businesses didn't end up as mature companies; they started out that way. The business was completely planned before it was begun. The owners see their job as working on the business instead of working in it. They had a model

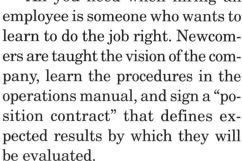

The mature business is more concerned with how things are done, as opposed to what is done.

in their minds of a business that was already working. It looked like the business they planned when they were through working on it. They see the business fulfilling the needs of a specific group of customers in an innovative way. The mature business is more concerned with how things are done, as opposed to what is done.

Each job or position must be described completely, even if only a few people operate the several positions of the business at the beginning. By describing each position – the work that needs to be done, the expectations for which each person at that position is held accountable, and who is accountable to whom – it is a simple matter to expand when needed.

All you need when hiring an employee is someone who wants to learn to do the job right. Newcomers are taught the vision of the company, learn the procedures in the operations manual, and sign a "position contract" that defines expected results by which they will be evaluated.

Rules for Franchise Models

Franchise models or systems that run consistently successful businesses follow these six rules, according to Gerber:

1. The model will provide consistent value to and exceed expectations of customers.

2. The model will be operated by people with the lowest possible level of skill.

3. The model will stand out as a place of impeccable order.

4. The work done in the model will be documented in operations manuals.

5. The model will provide a uniformly predictable product and/or service to the customer.

6. The model will use a uniform color, logo, dress and facilities code.

The most difficult of the rules to apply to the farrier business is No. 2 – the business is operated by people with the lowest possible levels of skill. If your model depends entirely on highly skilled people, it will be impossible to replicate. They are expensive and are difficult to hire and hold. Of course, we need people with farrier aptitude and some level of skills, but they don't have to be exceptional.

However, the system has to be exceptional to leverage ordinary people to produce extraordinary results. The system or "way of doing things" cannot be people- or expert-dependent. In fact, the most successful businesses are systems-dependent.

The solution to the problem in the 2nd rule is in the 4th rule. If we can accurately describe and write down what we want done (or what makes us skilled), then we have a better chance of communicating it to less-skilled workers. This process also helps us understand the skill better. A complete operations manual with checklists is essential for success. This structure provides order, which in turn provides the freedom to produce extraordinary results repeatedly.

The operations manual is a "How to Do It Guide" that designates the *purpose* of the work, describes step-by-step *procedures* of how to do the work, and specifies the *standards* expected for both the process and the results. (Descriptive standards for the horseshoeing job are found in Appendix 4.)

Choosing Employees

The most important qualification for an employee is not possessing skills but having a willingness to learn skills and become a part of your business dream or model. Maybe the employee is thrilled by the idea of apprenticeship. The more untrained or unspoiled the better. The single most important qualification for employees is the *desire to be part of your dream in a way* that gives consistency, order and predictability to both the customers and the workers. The process or system you set up orchestrates so consistency that everyone can depend on it, much like a well-rehearsed orchestra plays a symphony consistently at each performance. Like a great piece of well-played music, your business should create a mood.

Specifically, employees must be able and willing to follow directions. They must be willing to learn and grow into the business and become part of it. They love the joy of improving and competing against themselves, not others. They want to work toward being the best they can at the tasks they are accountable for.

After the thrill of apprenticeship passes, motivated people seek mastery of the craft at the level they are performing, then move to the next level, and so on. This keeps people growing and interested. They seek to become one with the work they create. As they reach the level of near-perfection, they become connected to themselves. They become craftsmen and love their work, and create with their whole soul as does the true artist. Mastery takes place over many years of orchestrated practice.

Saint Francis of Assisi wrote, "He who works with his hands is a laborer; he who works with his hands and his head is a craftsman; he who works with his hands, his head and his heart is an artist." As a craftsman approaches artistic mastery, he or she comes to know that the process of growing and changing is the root and foundation of mastery. Craftsmen feel connected to the past (apprenticeship), the present (work) and the future (legacy).

This is what business systems can do for us; they help us find ourselves and connect us to a meaning for our lives. Everything we know how to do is tested by what we don't know how to do. That conflict between the two creates growth, which in turn creates meaning.

Employees, whether they are Technicians or Managers, don't need to be professionals in the beginning. But they need to believe in predefined standards and want to learn how to do or manage them. The standards are the rules of the game. Each business needs its own rules that

Everything we know how to do is tested by what we don't know how to do. That conflict between the two creates growth, which in turn creates meaning.

are well understood and adhered to by all. Everything they do reflects your primary aim, which is the purpose of the business.

Gerber recommends making and honoring the rules of the "game." He suggests the following rules to get started on creating your own.

1. The Rules of the Game define what people do. The people (employees) do not define the rules or standards.

2. You must play the game before you can expect others to do it.

3. Make specific ways to win the game without ending it.

4. Change the game from time to time, but not the Primary Aim or Business Purpose.

5. Remind people of the game at least once a week; don't expect it to be self-sustaining.

6. The game has to make sense and be logical. (It must help people get what they want.)

7. The game needs to be fun from time-to-time; at least every six months.

8. If you can't think of a good game, borrow one and memorize it.

Research shows that the need to be encouraged, supported and recognized is usually more important than financial incentives. *The Wall Street Journal* says that, "Better than money, praise and personal gestures motivate workers. Things that don't cost money are ironically the most effective."

The Hiring Process

Hiring an employee is a difficult task at best. Dr. Brooks Mitchell has defined his views on employee selection in his book *Bet on Cowboys, Not Horses*. He has developed computer-administered questionnaires that help determine if a person is a "good hire" or not. Dr. Mitchell sums up what the person is looking for by saying, "I try to hire someone who is satisfied with his or her life in general, and who specifically will like the work required by the job for which they are applying." These will be people who "like doing what they're doing." He further says, "Feelings of boredom and monotony are not functions of the job, but more related to the make-up of a person's character."

How can you determine if people like their jobs? Do they want to do the work right? Ask them, and observe them before hiring. Some things are more important than other things to watch out for. There is a close relationship between high turnover, high theft, high absenteeism and low customer service. Any of these should throw up a red flag. Ask questions during the job interview that elicit the information you need. Learning their feelings about the ethical nature of a situation are most revealing. First impressions have been shown to be inaccurate and often cause us to miss important information. Always strive to hire the right person to start with.

Once a person is hired, a 60-day review has been shown to be particularly important. At a minimum, you should conduct a morale interview at 60 days to solidify the hiring process. Before that time, employees should be understood to be probationary.

Selection of employees is important. Biographical information has a much greater predictability of performance than intelligence, ability, aptitude or personality. Research shows that human character doesn't change on the job and, according to Dr. Mitchell, "Anybody who believes it does should be working for social services, not a for-profit business." Offering training programs is not as important as knowing who you have to train. Past behavior represents the best predictor of future behavior. People tend to develop a fairly stable style of life comprised of a set of values, principles and behavior patterns. Human behav-

ior is, for the most part, repetitive.

To reduce the level of stress in hiring and increase the possibility of getting one who is willing to play the game of your business well, you need to realize:

1. Employees are important; they make a difference.

2. Employees can't be transformed; you must hire right.

3. People who work with the employee must take responsibility for hiring.

4. The hiring decision can be made more effectively with a structured interview.

5. Scoring of the interview must come from measured, job-specific criteria.

6. Interview questions need to be open-ended, i.e., "How will your plans for future education be affected by your employment with us?" This is preferred, rather than asking, "Are you planning to go to school?"

The secret to having productive employees is to hire the right person, and then manage the job, not the person. A bad employee will contaminate your business. Always check references and ask for additional references when interviewing those listed by the prospective employee. People who over-respond on an application or in an interview and tell you what you want to hear usually make bad hires, according to Dr. Mitchell.

Systems and Scripts Needed

You need systems standards and scripts for each part of the job. In short, you need an Operations Manual so when you are not present, people can still carry on and make the business work.

One way to do this in a horseshoeing business is to stagger your apprentices. One should be nearly as experienced as the master and others on lower levels. For example, if there are four apprentices, one has four years experience, one has three, one has two, and one is in the first year. This is a common arrangement in Europe and Great Britain, but rare in America.

Each person should have a job description and know his or her duties. Descriptions should be reviewed at least weekly, along with a reminder about the purpose of the business, improvements to be implemented, and promises the customer wants to hear – promises that set us apart because we can make them and no one else can!

> *The secret to having productive employees is to hire the right person, and then manage the job, not the person.*

Inventory, scheduling, policies (such as shoe replacement, dealing with bad horses, etc.) and financial systems should all be in place.

In summary, if we work on our business so that it will provide what we want in life, we must devise systems and put them in place. The process of business development creates changes in the people who do it. The business becomes a symbol for the life they wish to live, a visible manifestation of who they are and what they believe.

You must analyze your business as it is, then decide what it will look like when it is finally the way you want it. After that, determine what you must do to make your dream a reality. It is not until we apply these ideas that we begin to understand them and comprehend what we've been missing all this time.

Defining a Well-Managed Practice

Being well managed means making a good profit while making client service a top priority. The best practices, farrier or veterinary, have several things in common, according to Cyntha Wutcheitt, CPA, from Columbus, Ohio.

1. Patients (horses) always come first. Focus is on the best interests or welfare of the horse. Service with sensible skill is the basis of success.

2. Efficiency is more important than size or revenue. Ratio of profit to total revenue is most important. Net profit after paying variable, fixed and overhead costs should be between 40% and 45% of total revenue.

3. As business owners, how we feel about ourselves and what we do affects our relationships toward our employees and our clients. This in turn affects the quality of service we can offer and directly affects client retention. Owners of successful practices constantly look for ways to improve.

A 1998 study of well-managed veterinary practices by Wutcheitt and Associates, showed that growth depended on five key trends. These can be applied to farrier businesses as well. Ongoing success depends on the ability to:

1. Compensate business owners for time, knowledge and experience.

2. Increase clients' perception of value of services offered.

3. Systematically provide high quality, affordable medical care.

4. Increase staff members' contributions to bottom-line revenue.

5. Build market share in the community.

Incorporating these factors into your business plans and building systems to implement them will position you for success, even in a highly competitive environment.

Liability Issues

Liability lawsuits have increased dramatically in America in recent years. You need to do all in your power to limit your liability while working, and protect yourself with liability insurance. Here are some tips on limiting your liability exposure.

1. Screen owners or employers more closely than horses. Work only for clients who realize that accidents can happen, and that these accidents are no one's fault but may result from risk that is inherent when owning and working with horses. It is the owner's responsi-

bility to present a well-trained and safe animal for shoeing.

2. If the animal is not receptive to being worked on, it is the owner's responsibility to obtain a veterinarian to administer chemical restraint or have the horse trained using physical restraint. If you are asked to train the animal, do so only in a safe area and charge a training fee in addition to the shoeing fee. If the owner appears unwilling to do this, it is the farrier's responsibility to deny service to the client's horse(s).

3. Keep a daily log of what occurred at each appointment. Record such things as the behavior of the horse, the behavior and statements made by the owner or recommendations you have made, the type and dimensions of the shoe used and the conditions under which the work was done. This information could be recorded on a dictaphone or tape recorder between appointments and transcribed later into a daybook or contact management software notepad.

4. Have a witness other than the owner present when working on an animal that may be a problem. This person could perform the duties of a holder and verify your statements of what transpired on a given occasion.

5. Take training and certification tests to the highest level possible. This helps to show you are a professional and may be valuable in establishing your position in a court case. Go to as many continuing education programs as possible. Network with fellow professionals who may be able to help you in a court case by letter or by appearance.

6. Stop work immediately when the situation becomes dangerous or impossible. We all like to finish what we start, but this may not be wise in some cases. When you don't feel safe or good about what you are doing, stop. It is the owner's responsibility to provide a safe environment in which to work. If clients seem to be unconcerned for your safety, you don't have to work for them.

7. Use a tool bag, not a toolbox, when working on a difficult horse. If the horse falls, steps in it or kicks at the tools, there will be less chance of injury to the horse or farrier. Insist that children be kept at a distance and dogs be tied up when you are working.

8. Insure yourself with comprehensive liability insurance to protect from unforeseen situations, unreasonable people or unruly animals. Don't discuss the extent of this coverage with your clients.

9. Remain in control of yourself at all times. If you feel you are losing control, stop immediately and get away from the condition(s) until your composure returns.

10. Do what you can to protect yourself by wearing safety equipment, such as glasses, hearing protection, steel-toed boots, knee pads or supports, wrist supports and back support. Exercise regularly. Schedule frequent short vacations. Think safety in your work area for you, the horse and the client.

11. Make a brochure that explains your policies and fees to the client or potential client. Follow the practices consistently as they are outlined. If you don't intend to follow them literally, don't put them in the brochure. Be sure your behavior and your written policies are consistent. Express and follow guidelines that separate the duties of a farrier, veterinarian and horse trainer. Avoid doing anything that could be construed as veterinary medicine.

12. Be positive in your outlook and daily contacts, but be cautious in your commitments and in the performance of your service. Express empathy and sympathy for accidents that may occur. Accept responsibility for those that are clearly your fault.

13. Have more than one skill and income. Don't depend solely on your farrier income, so you can say "no" to unfavorable conditions. Save and invest money. Economize.

14. Manage your farrier business like a business. Obtain the advice of com-

petent legal counsel and financial planners. Organize your business to limit your liability exposure.

Business Entities

An important part of establishing systems is organizing your business into an entity that gives you maximum tax advantages and minimum liability exposure. Normally, it is best to use the simplest form of business available for your circumstances. The chart on the following page briefly compares business entities.

You should get the advice of an accountant and an attorney to help you decide which one is best for you. "Pass through" refers to income (or loss) passed through the business and federally taxed at the personal level. "Perpetual business life" refers to the ability to transfer business ownership to buyer(s) or heir(s).

Business Entities

Business Structure	Ownership	Pros and Cons
Sole proprietorship	One person	Pass through, easy to set up, some expenses not deductible, liability exposure unlimited.
Partnership	Two or more persons, may be a syndicate.	Pass through, flexible allocation of profit and loss, liability exposure unlimited.
Limited-liability partnership	Two or more persons.	Pass through, some tax flexibility, liability limited to original invest ment, not accepted in all states.
Limited-liability company	Flexible number of "members" and proportion.	Pass through, some tax flexibility, cost of switching to corporations is high, limited liability, differs from state to state.
"S" Corporation	Shareholders, limited stock and voting rights.	Pass through, easy to set up, limits financing, some expenses not deductible, limited liability, perpetual business life.
"C" Corporation	Shareholders, unlimited stock and voting rights.	Income, losses and deductions taxed at lower corporate levels, may result in "double taxation," costly to set up and maintain, officer and employee benefits deductible, limited liability, perpetual business life.

Chapter 9

How to Organize and Financially Plan for Your Future

Chapter 9

How to Organize and Financially Plan for Your Future

If We Fail To Plan

Typically, when we are young, we think we are indestructible. As we get older, our perspective changes. The sooner we start to make decisions and take action regarding financial planning for the future, the better off we will be. The sun shines tomorrow on those who plan ahead and make the right decisions today. And the opposite is also true. If we fail to plan, we are planning to fail when future storms come into our lives.

The Social Security Administration's research says that at age 65, 45% of Americans are dependent on relatives, 30% are dependent on charity and 23% are still working while only 2% are self-sustaining. According to J. Arthur Ureivoli of Merrill Lynch, today's average 50-year-old has only $2,300 saved toward retirement. A recent study found that 93% of men at age 65 who have failed financially gave "failure to plan" as the reason for their situation.

It's not how much you make that's important. It's how much you can keep that counts. I met a horseshoer from California who told me he had made over a million dollars shoeing horses, but he said, "I have nothing to show for it now." How can we prevent that from happening to us?

Financial Planning

Ideally, financial planning begins early in your career. It should be reviewed and revised each time you experience a major change in your business or personal life. Your financial plan will affect the type of business structure you choose. (See the end of Chapter 8 for a comparison.) Changes in federal or state tax laws may also affect your financial plan.

Lack of planning for tax consequences could result in up to a 55% federal estate tax bite within 90 days of your death. This reality could be devastating to your family.

One of the most important things you can do is to select an advisor. These people should be certified and come to you well recommended. Your banking and/or insurance partners often can be of help in this area. Most have staff members trained in this field.

Even with an advisor, it's still important to study and learn the basics of financial planning, since *only you* can decide how to best protect and provide for you and your family. Think of your financial planner as a resource and advisor. He or she can be one of your most valuable partners in business. Let financial advisors and planners help you, but don't turn the responsibility for doing it completely over to them. You may regret it.

Because our population is living longer, many Americans spend as much time in retirement as they did in their careers. As well, people are increasingly required to take more responsibility for health care. That requires having financial resources for years after retirement.

Retirement is one future need, but there are others. For example, the rising cost of higher education continues to outpace inflation. According to a recent article in *The Wall Street Journal*, the average cost at public colleges and universities is $7,773 a year; for private institutions, it is $20,273 a year. Considering it takes five years for the average student to graduate, the expense is great.

Good financial planning makes these and other future dreams possible for your family. A comprehensive financial plan helps you organize a network of professionals so you can get better control of your future finances.

Having A Will

Everyone should have a will. But, according to the February 24, 2000 issue of *USA Today*, most people under the age of 44 don't have one. The percentages drop as people get older. About 59% of Americans 35 to 44 years of age don't have a will, while the number is 37% for people 45 to 54 and 38% for people 55 to 64. For those over 65, 25% don't have a will.

In most states, when a person dies without a will, the state decides who receives the property belonging to the deceased. Also, property can be tied up in probate for an extended period of time. Probate is the official proving of authenticity of a will in court.

Once you have a will, it rarely needs to be changed unless: 1) you change your mind on the administration and distribution of property, or 2) you change your state of residence. A codicil, or amendment, can be used in some cases when you want to make simple changes.

Living wills have become popular in recent years. A living will is often used to declare your wishes in case you become unconscious and/or are unable to make your wishes known concerning extended life support. There are also durable powers of attorney that authorize others to make decisions for you in special circumstances.

Arranging A Trust

Many trust arrangements make good sense to use in estate planning. Trusts, like wills, can help make property transition easier after death by avoiding long and costly probate. Trusts can administer money to children for education or business start-up. They can defer taxes but not avoid them. A legitimate trust is a legal form of estate planning. It's best to see an attorney specializing in trusts when you are ready to set one up.

Recently, the appeal of trusts has been promoted in the form of what the Internal Revenue Service (IRS) calls "abusive trusts." Beware whenever you hear promises to hide ownership of assets and income with the objective of avoiding taxes. Some names for these abusive trusts may include: business trust, equipment trust or service trust, family residence trust, charitable organization trust and final foreign trust.

According to the American Horse Council, the IRS has "undertaken a nationally coordinated enforcement initiative" to crack down on salespeople promoting these trusts as well as those buyers contacted by the promoters. Since most taxpayers desire to pay fewer taxes – and it is widely believed that the rich can avoid taxes – the appeal is strong, and con men play off of it. The aura of exclusivity and secrecy associated with trusts fuels the appeal for tax avoidance. In reality, if is sounds too good to be true, it probably is. What's more, involvement in these entities often triggers audits.

Getting Insurance

Working at a dangerous job like horseshoeing without some kind of accident insurance is foolish. While it is true that farrier organizations and good-hearted people have helped injured farriers in need, you shouldn't depend on this charity. I know from personal experience that one accident can run up a bill you can never hope to pay without insurance coverage. Many associations offer special discounts to members with participating insurance companies.

Compare benefits thoroughly when purchasing medical insurance. Usually, the larger the deductible or the amount you copay to activate the coverage, the lower the premium. You can even get credit for putting this money in a medical savings account for this purpose. Beware of low ceiling limits on coverage since medical care is so expensive, even for the short-term. And costs for long-term care are astronomical.

Life insurance is needed most when you are rearing a family and paying a mortgage on a home. You should compare whole life and term life insurance to see which type works best for you. The rule of thumb is to have at least three times your annual income as a life insurance benefit amount.

Liability insurance has almost become a necessity in this day and age. You should carry it, but do not discuss that you have it with your clients. Sometimes, you can obtain this insurance most inexpensively through an independent agent in conjunction with other business insurance. However, it may be best to get it through your trade association. Be sure you understand exactly what is covered and what is not. Then conduct your business in a professional manner, as negligence is not defensible.

Disability insurance is a difficult call. Chances are, if you are injured seriously, you would be unable to work. Disability insurance is designed to replace income during convalescent periods. This type of insurance is frequently abused and therefore carries a relatively high premium. It offers many levels of protection. Each case must be considered individually.

If you have employees, workman's compensation is normally required.

Savings and Investments

Saving at least 10% of your income and investing it in growth-yielding ways has been recommended since the beginning of time. *The Richest Man in Babylon*

by George S. Clason contains an old story that teaches a universal truth about making sure you keep a part of all you earn by paying yourself first. This requires self-discipline and an adjustment in your standard of living, which is probably why so few do it. But this attitude, when executed, pays off.

The payoff resulting from the magic of compound interest on your savings and investments gets your attention when you see your money double. You can figure out how long it will take by using the rule of 72. When you invest money, divide 72 by the annual rate of return to find the approximate number of years it takes to double your money. For example at 6%, it takes 12 years to double your money (72 ÷ 6 = 12).

The rule of leverage is another way you can make your money work for you. This involves buying property with a low down payment such as 10% of purchase price instead of paying the full price. For example, if you buy a $100,000 property and it appreciates 5%, you earned $5,000. However, if you paid a 10% down payment, you are leveraged at 10 to 1 and now will make 10 x 5% or 50% or $50,000. Some real estate investors earn rates of 25% to 50% using this technique. A strong real estate market can allow you to do this, too.

The famed movie character Forrest Gump said, "I'm not a smart man, but I know what love is." Here is another truth: "It doesn't take a smart man to make money, but it takes a smart one to keep it."

One of my earliest horseshoeing students was a city kid who wanted to make it big. He worked hard and did his best to excel at everything I taught him. He was not naturally talented; everything came hard for him. But he had persistence. Several years later, I heard from him. He thanked me for sticking with him in his training and told me he had become quite successful shoeing racehorses, traveling from track to track. I didn't hear from him again for 30 years. A few years ago, he came to see me and told me his life story. It was most instructive.

He had made several million dollars in his lifetime of shoeing horses. He had owned several expensive homes and had traveled around the world. But his style of living had extracted its toll. His spirits were low; his net worth was gone. His sole possession was an old car and small camp trailer. All of his "wealth" had evaporated. His future looked bleak. Sadly, he regretted he was not smart enough to keep his money and invest it wisely.

> *Here is another truth: "It doesn't take a smart man to make money, but it takes a smart one to keep it."*

Most financial planners recommend a diversification of investments. One example suggested by a well-known financial planner calls for dividing your funds into these categories: 60% in capital preservation such as real estate, money market, certificates of deposit and bonds; 25% in growth and income mutual funds and preferred stocks; 15% in growth and higher risk funds such as consistent growth companies and a few start-ups.

The rate of return can be expected to increase as the risk increases. However, the 15% invested in the more risky stock market should be money you can afford to lose. Capital preservation might return 6%, growth and income investments 8% to 10%, growth and risk stocks 12% to 15%. These may fluctuate even less in the short term. According to a study by the Harvard School of Business, less than 1% of the people who trade stocks frequently actually make money. Remember, time in the market is more important than timing the market.

The following two ways help you accumulate money over time if you start when you are young. One is to invest a large sum such as $10,000 when you are 30

105

and let it grow by reinvesting the interest income it generates every year. At 15% interest compounded annually, you will have $1.3 million by age 65. Another way is to invest $1,000 each year from the age of 30 to age 65 and let it grow by reinvesting annual income. At 15% interest compounded annually, you will have $1 million by age 65.

At Age 30 . . .
$2,000 per year earning 10%
for 35 years = $596,253.62
Total amount invested $70,000
Income earned $526,253.62

At Age 40 . . .
$2,000 per year earning 10%
for 25 years = $216,363.53
Total amount invested $50,000
Income earned $166,363.53

At Age 50 . . .
$2,000 per year earning 10%
for 15 years = $69,899.46
Total amount invested $30,000
Income earned $39,899.46

Retirement Plans

Retirement plans are investments that combine the principle of saving for the future with a built-in protection against inflation through investments. In addition, there is a tax deferment provision to some of the plans approved by the IRS. That means taxes owed on interest earned do not have to be paid until later in life. Your accountant can advise you on these.

Each of the Individual Retirement Accounts (IRAs) are different in their tax consequences and ability to meet your special needs. Study them carefully.

The contribution to most people's retirement funding from the U.S. government through Social Security is very small. It certainly has not kept pace with inflation, so don't depend on it for all your living expenses.

According to a 1996 Shoeing Practices Survey reported in the November 1997 issue of *AFJ*, of the 60% of full-time farrriers who report having a retirement account, 50% say they have an IRA, 23% have a Keogh/self-employed pension plan. Some have more than one. These plans typically invest in certificates of deposit, stocks and mutual funds. The numbers reported in November 1998 are even lower.

The Simple IRA (1996) and the Roth IRA (1997) are both potentially useful tools for farriers. As of 2001, the Simple IRA allows a maximum of $6,500 (employee deferral plus 2-3% employer matching) to be invested each year with the taxes deferred until the money is taken out. The key to success, as with all retirement plans, is time; the longer funds are left in, generally the more will be accumulated as a nest egg. What's more, the tax savings may be significant in your peak earning years.

The Roth IRA does not give the tax deferment benefit, but does provide for IRA funds to be tax-free at retirement. Only $2,000 can be put into a Roth each year in addition to transferred funds. Persons with lower income and tax brackets may benefit more from the Roth than the Simple. Check with your tax adviser about your situation. IRS laws change from year to year.

Other types of retirement choices are the SEP and 401(k) plans. Talk to your financial advisor and explore the best choice and mix for you. Most do not recommend annuities. Some encourage investing in real estate, apartment houses and other "stable" businesses instead of using standard retirement plans. The important thing is to have a plan or some combination of plans and the self-discipline to fund it (them).

Author H.G. Wells once said, "Wealth, notoriety, place and power are no measure of success whatever. The only true measure of success is the ratio between what we might have done and what we might have been on the one hand, and the thing we have made of ourselves on the other."

Chapter 10

How to Position and Market Your Business

Chapter 10

How to Position and Market Your Business

Purpose of Business

The purpose of a business is to create and keep customers. In order to do this, each customer or client must perceive value in the services provided.

In effect, clients have us do their work because they trust us. What is trust? It involves many interconnected values:

- Trust is character plus competency.

- Character equals honesty and goodness.

- Competency equals skill plus character.

- Skill equals accuracy plus speed.

- Character is something that can be felt; competency is something that is tested.

- Self-esteem or self-confidence must be present in order to practice professionally.

- Self-esteem comes from confidence in competence and product, along with a concentrated business focus.

- More training and constant striving for improvement, added to learned experience, results in increased confidence.

Marketing Products and Services

There are two major ways to market products and services. One is by purposefully positioning a business in the client's mind; the other is to influence the client to change his or her mind about the business.

You can use a variety of strategies to make your business goals and objectives come to pass. To get started, I suggest you respond to the questions outlined in the chart below. This exercise helps you determine your specific competitive advantage in the area where you work.

The following chart is adapted from *Market Smarter, Not Harder* by M.R. Myron and P. Truax. This book is highly recommended to help you understand marketing as it applies to your business.

Marketing Strategies for Farriers

Adapted with permission from *Market Smarter, Not Harder* by M. R. Myron and P. Truax

Questions for Evaluation	Specific Action Plans
Competitive Strategies	1. Competitive Strategies
1. How many similar-sized farrier businesses are in your area?	
2. When a new competitor comes into your area, do you experience a slow, eroding loss of business, or a sudden decrease in customers? How can you prevent any loss?	
• Be certain to differentiate your product or farrier services according to what customers want. • Be clear about the problem(s) you solve or benefit(s) you have to offer.	
Target Market Strategies	2. Target Market Strategies
1. How do you differentiate your farrier business among others in your primary target market?	
2. Do you market to the horse owner or the trainer? Why?	
3. What is different about your competitors' target market compared to yours?	
4. Is there potential in other target markets you are not currently serving?	
• Be sure to communicate your message to your target market. • Determine if it's wise to expand your target market.	
Product/Service Strategies	3. Product/Service Strategies
1. How will you market new products or services?	
2. Which products or services will you focus on more than others?	
3. Is your goal to increase repeat purchases?	
4. How might production or the cost of producing a product change?	
• Determine any global or marketplace factors (economic conditions, politics, environmental concerns) that would affect production. • Decide if it's more cost-effective to buy wholesale or buy in quantity.	

Questions for Evaluation	Specific Action Plans

Pricing Strategies

4. Pricing Strategies

1. How does your pricing rank with that of your competitors?

2. Is your pricing too high or too low by comparison?

3. Does your pricing need to change to be more competitive?

4. If it is higher than what competitors offer, do you clearly give customers a reason (added value) to pay more?

  - Price is the value you demand for your product or service.
  - Pros sell value, amateurs sell price.

Positioning Strategies

5. Positioning Strategies

1. Do you expect immediate results or do you focus on long-term image?

2. Does your message clearly communicate benefits?

3. Is your message effective for your target market(s)?

4. Is your positioning consistent with your price?

5. Does your positioning differ from that of your competitors?

6. Is your positioning reflected in all print and broadcast materials?

  - Positioning is the place your product or service occupies in the mind of your prospects and customers.
  - Use your positioning statement to develop a positioning strategy.

Promotion Strategies

6. Promotion Strategies

1. How many of your past promotions were successful?

2. Did you track the results of these promotions?

3. What successful promotions do your competitors use?

4. How can you create a joint promotion with farrier suppliers, feed stores or companies, thus reducing costs while providing additional coverage?

5. Is promotion a consistent part of your plan, or is it event driven?

  - Short-term promotional strategies aim to influence target market buyer behavior during a specific period to achieve a targeted amount of revenue.
  - Look for creative ways to offer promotions jointly.
  - Track results and learn from your mistakes.

Questions for Evaluation	Specific Action Plans
Public Relations Strategies	7. Public Relations Strategies

Public Relations Strategies

1. Do you have a public relations plan?

2. How much time can you allocate to developing public relations?

3. What is unique about your products or farrier services that would interest the media?

4. Through what publications and other media can you reach people in your target market?

5. How can public relations benefit your advertising and marketing strategies?

- Well-placed public relations can be more effective than paid advertising because they imply endorsement by an unbiased third party.
- Media people are always looking for interesting material.

Implementation Calendar

Next, you will want to put together an implementation calendar you can use to plan and track your results with the marketing objectives and strategies you have put together. This calendar can also be used to plan and track how you will spend your marketing dollars to generate new business and show appreciation to existing customers. This is important, since the majority of your business will be repeat business and new business will come from referrals. You will soon see that individual customers have great value over the life of your business. You need to treat them well.

You will soon see that individual customers have great value over the life of your business. You need to treat them well.

Create an image for your business that is consistent with the goals you have set for yourself. This can include a statement that identifies what benefits a customer receives from doing business with you. Using an attractive card, invoice, business sign and stationery plus wearing appropriate clothing are all helpful.

What is Positioning?

Positioning refers to where your business is "located" in the mind of the customer compared with others who have similar products and services. If you don't understand these principles of positioning and use them in your business, your competitors may gain an advantage over you. Patricia Fripp, a popular business speaker, has said, "The only thing I ever wanted in business was an unfair advantage." That's what we all want.

To create something that doesn't already exist in the customer's mind is becoming more and more difficult according to Jack Trout in his book *The New Positioning*. We have become an over-communicated society. Over half of the jobs in the U.S. are information-related occupations. The only hope for your message to be heard is to concentrate on narrow, simplified targets. Millions of dollars have been wasted trying to change minds. But the truth is, the average person can't stand to be told he or she is wrong. People's minds are already "made up."

Positioning is the only answer to the problems of marketing in an over-communicated society. With so many forms of media available to sell messages, we use as many as practical. Even your body can become an advertising billboard, i.e., the type of shirts and hats you wear. Professionals and institutions actively advertise. Even the government spends billions on advertising.

Positioning is a tactic for finding a window into the mind. The easiest way to get into the mind is to be first. First is better than best. Get there first, and be careful not to give customers a reason to switch. Be a big fish in a small pond rather than a little fish in a big pond. One way to success is to look at what your competitors are doing, and then subtract the "poetry" or "creativity" that has become the barrier to getting the message into someone's mind. With a simplified message, you can then penetrate your prospect's mind and the prospect gets what he or she expects to see.

> *The easiest way to get into the mind is to be first. First is better than best.*

According to Harvard psychologist Dr. George A. Miller, the average human cannot deal with more than seven units at a time. Ranking things is a convenient way to keep from being overwhelmed by the complexities of life.

Simplifying your message means that less is more. Use simplification to sharpen all your messages as you place your solution in the prospect's mind. Remember that perception is reality. Very little information gets through from the outside to the inside. What does get through will be the simple, memorable truths.

Coming to grips with the competition is the main challenge in most marketing situations. The secret to establishing a successful position is to keep these two concepts in balance: the unique position combined with an appeal that is not too narrow. Select a position no one else has firmly gripped. Define yourself as a specialist.

Being First Is Better Than Best

To be successful, the best strategy is to relate to others. Learn to link yourself with a name already in the mind of the prospect, such as the use of the name, _Un Cola_. Don't forget what made you successful. Advertise your achievements, not your aspirations. Pay attention to your competitors' positions and your own.

Realistically, there are limits on everything: timing, finances, reach, in wrong part of the cycle. If we are out of phase, we will not succeed. Be realistic. If you didn't get in at the right time, recognize you can't catch up. Find a viable alternative position to the leaders. To be a leader, you must be "firstest with the mostest."

History has shown that the first brand gets twice the long-term market share of number two. And two gets twice as much as three, and the relationships among them aren't easily changed. An example of applying this to shoeing is competition from the "natural" fad. The "natural" idea is used to sell every conceivable product from vitamins to running shoes. As a strategy, you can compete by positioning yourself as "unnatural." Shoes are unnatural but necessary. Riding horses is unnatural and shoeing is necessary if we are going to use horses as domestic animals.

Customers are somewhat like chickens – they feel much more comfortable with a pecking order that everyone knows about and accepts. When the situation is in doubt, that is the time for extra effort. Like chickens establishing a pecking order, a lot of effort at first often makes the difference for years to come. Here's an analogy: it takes 110% of the rated power of a jet to get the plane off the ground but only 70% of its power to cruise at 600 mph at 30,000 miles altitude.

I believe it's better to enhance value of all horseshoers and foot care providers than to say you are number one. Either the prospect knows you are number one or wonders why you are so insecure you have to say so!

Like chickens establishing a pecking order, a lot of effort at first often makes the difference for years to come.

Additional Positioning Strategies

People take names very literally. Much thought and testing should go into the name of your business for it's the hook that hangs a perception in the prospect's mind. The single most important decision is what to name your business or product. Don't use initials as a name until you are famous.

Specifically, look for open positions or "holes" in the prospect's mind. Separate greed from opportunity when going after the high-priced market. Charging higher prices will not work unless you are: 1) the first to establish the high-price position, 2) the first to have a valid product story, or 3) the first to be in a category where consumers are receptive to a high-priced brand. If these conditions aren't met, your high price will just drive customers away. Clearly position yourself in a particular price category, making price a feature of the product. Raise prices only to new customers at first, or make a significant raise for them and a smaller one for old, reliable customers. Find special ways to treat them both.

Don't be all things to all people. Try to state why they shouldn't use competitor products or services, like aspirin versus Tylenol. Get people to change their minds about the competitor's product. Clearly point out the benefits of yours.

Make the most of every minute of your 15 minutes of fame. The most difficult part of positioning is to select one specific concept to hang your hat on. Ability and hard work are not all that counts. Instead, find a "horse" to ride: a company, boss, friend, idea, faith, yourself. And find a way to hook your product, service or concept to what is already in the prospect's mind.

In summary, positioning is the place you own in a person's mind (first, best, most colorful, etc.). You must first look for a place not occupied, then go for it by comparing yourself against the competition. Usually, that means being a specialist, not a generalist. Focus on the problem, not goals or objectives. It's not a matter of what you deserve or what is right; it's a matter of perception. The more practical and successful way to achieve goals is to deal with perceptions. Look for the specific (as it is perceived) and then generalize it. Your service or product can only mean *one* thing – not *all* things – to the customer.

The most difficult part of positioning is to select one specific concept to hang your hat on.

The Value (Power) of Simplicity

Business people have gone the way of university-manufactured professions by adopting and inventing all sorts of "buzz" words to describe common sense, everyday activities. For example, a vet might use the verbiage "Subluxation of the distal phalanx" when "dislocation of the coffin bone" would work better. Or a farrier says the horse is "rank" when he or she means it could hurt you. The purpose of these charades is similar to that of "professors" and "professions," serving to exclude outsiders from understanding their encrypted messages. They are sure these pompous words will make them look smart, a result valued by them much more than the virtues of common sense and hard work. These people must be very insecure to want to create complexity and distance themselves from ordinary people. In ancient times, this was done in the royal courts – people learned foreign languages or "dead" languages so they could be separate from the common people.

The reality of life is that clear, tough-minded people are the most simple and successful ones. People seem to fear being simple – especially those who have had the opportunity for education.

Said Peter Drucker in his book *Power of Simplicity,* "People in the past often tried to make a secret of knowledge because it is powerful. Today, power comes from transmitting information to make it productive, not from hiding it."

Lessons in Simplicity

Here is a simple list of attitudes to adopt to bring simplicity into your life.

- Never let a confusing word or concept go unchallenged.

- Be intolerant of intellectual arrogance.

- Your first impressions are often the most accurate.

- Never trust anyone you don't understand.

- Big ideas almost always come in small words.

- It's not age that causes memory lapse, it's information overload. Our "discs" are full.

- You're a decision maker, not an information expert. Prioritize. Delegate.

- Don't give your e-mail address or cell-phone number to everyone.

- Escape from technology for a short time daily.

- If you unclutter your mind, you will think more clearly.

- Advertise your material as simple and to the point. Convey *simple sensible solutions.*

Value Versus Price

The consultant's view is that companies won't pay a lot for simplicity. In fact, the less a company (or a person) understands a process (or a disease) the more it will pay. But in reality, it is all about doing the right thing, not the fashionable thing. Don't waste energy and resources by creating unrealistic expectations and undermining client confidence.

In real estate, it is location, location, location. In business, it is differentiate, differentiate, differentiate. Supply your customers with a reason to buy from you instead of your competitors. Differentiate by making yourself unique through your unique selling point or USP as noted by Rosser Reeves in *Reality in Advertising*. Look for weak points in positions of competitors, and then make yourself different.

- If you are not different, you better have a low price.

- There is no such thing as an untapped market.

- Customers are strongly or weakly held by competitors.

- Treat customers well so they buy more and complain less.

- It's not about knowing your customer – it's about your customer knowing you.

- A thing is worth whatever the buyer will pay for it and your competition will let you charge.

  – Pubilius Syrus,
  Roman writer,
  1st century B.C.

- Put your money where the opportunities *are* – not where they *were*.

- New entrants get established on price.

- Marking up prices only works if your competition follows you.

- Ask yourself if all this theory is nonsense or if it is brilliance buried in complexity.

- Nothing is more simple than greatness; indeed, to be simple is to be great.

  – Ralph Waldo Emerson

First Impressions

First impressions last. A person calling your business forms an opinion in the first four-to-six seconds. Every person who speaks on the phone represents your business. Train whoever answers the phone, including yourself, to do these important things:

- Answer with the company name and a friendly greeting.

- Answer with a smile that can be heard.

- Treat each call individually with anticipation. Avoid negative words or phrases.

- Get the essential information needed by asking questions that fill in the blanks.

- When making calls, if a person doesn't answer, be prepared to leave a brief, upbeat message. Ask when it is best for you to call back. *The Wall Street Journal* reports only 30% of all business calls get completed on the first try. Make every call count.

- Return all calls within 24 hours, or sooner if possible.

- Be courteous and caring, even if you are not feeling well. Sometimes, you may have to "fake" it a bit.

Techniques of Persuasion

In my experience, there are two parts to marketing. One is positioning or finding that site in the customer's mind that is not occupied with another product or service. Two is to use the psychology of persuasion to promote a product or service by changing the customer's mind.

Dr. Robert Cialdini calls this the psychology of compliance or "the weapons of influence." He has identified six powerful weapons in his book *Influence – The Psychology of Persuasion* that cause automatic reactions in people. Each "weapon" has the ability to produce a "mindless compliance," that is, an obligation to give a "yes" response without thinking. He compares the instinctive behavior in animals to these characteristics of humans.

The weapons of influence are powerful and used by all knowledgeable advertising persons. These techniques are especially well understood among dishonest people or con men. Be aware of them to protect yourself as well as use them to influence others.

People are preoccupied with their own self-interest. They will always look for the best value, which will not always be sold at the lowest price. The best perceived value always wins. The weapons of influence that create an automatic response include reciprocation, consistency, social proof, liking, authority and scarcity. Let's discuss what each of these rules mean and how you can apply them in marketing your business.

1. Reciprocation

We feel compelled to repay, in kind, what another has provided for us. We feel obligated to or in debt to another. Gifts or favors elicit repayment or concessions. The typical technique is to give a gift before asking for a donation or sale. The free sample to try "without cost or obligation" causes us to want to buy to return the favor.

Our best defense against the reciprocation weapon is to refuse to accept gifts or privileges.

Yet how can we use this reciprocation to promote our horseshoeing business? We can give free literature, hoof picks and other useful articles to clients. Preferably, the business name will be noted on the token to keep it in front of the clients so they will refer more work to us. Your proven ambassadors (people who recommend you often) could be given more expensive gifts, such as books, hats, coffee cups and grooming tools. In this way, we keep the name and the purpose of the business in front of the client.

Bob Schantz of Foristell, Missouri, is quoted in the November, 1999, *American Farriers Journal:*

"When he was shoeing full-time, Bob Schantz liked to present clients with a video or book during the holiday season. 'Bob Miller's videos on imprinting foals makes a super present for owners, even if they only have one horse,' says the operator of the Spanish Lake Blacksmith Shop in Foristell, Missouri. 'The handling work that they do with their horses will come back many times over in the video investment you've made because of the time it will save during shoeing.'"

"For bigger accounts, Schantz presented Doug Butler's book *The Principles of Horseshoeing II.* 'This is an expensive gift, but the investment can pay off in spades,' says Schantz. 'After they've read it and referred to it, barn managers have a much better appreciation of what you are trying to do with their horses. They will also be much more knowledgeable about shoeing techniques.'"

2. Consistency

We feel compelled to support something we have committed to even if we don't want to, in order to be consistent. Consistency is a highly valued character trait.

Our best defense against this weapon is to avoid committing to things we don't want to do in the first place. When we get a feeling the proposal is not something we want to do, we must act and say no. If we comply with the first request, we tend to comply with the next one. After being set up to be taken advantage of, we are wise to ask this: "Knowing what I know now, would I make the same choice again?" Obey your first impression.

How can we use this weapon in horseshoeing? Ask questions regarding the persons' level of commitment to caring for their horse(s). If they say they want the horse done at a regular interval, they will be very reluctant to withdraw that commitment later. Surveys are great tools to get people to commit to things they wouldn't ordinarily commit to before asking for a sale. People who keep up their other property usually keep up and spend money to take care of their horses.

3. Social Proof

We feel compelled to accept ideas that a great number of people accept. We think the greater the number of people who find any idea correct, the more likely the idea will be correct. People are more persuaded by the actions of others than any other proof we can offer. Uncertainty draws us to conformity, or into action or inaction.

Our best defense against this weapon is to recognize when the underlying data, premise or principle is in error. There are two ways incorrect data occurs. One is a falsification of the data. Some-times this is obvious, sometimes not. But, once recognized, we should withdraw support.

Another is the realization that our thinking may be faulty to believe that others know what is good for us. We'd often be better off to think for ourselves. Con persons don't encourage us to think for ourselves. They are often recognized when they say one thing and do another. Watch what people do. Hypocrisy, the opposite of integrity, is a dominant characteristic of these folks.

How can we use this weapon in our horseshoeing business? The fads that we see being introduced into our industry are largely started and supported by social proof. It is difficult to get people to think for themselves. Trust helps people listen to you. Influencing others to accept your ideas, service policies and preferred products can be encouraged by reports and testimonials of other satisfied customers. Names and pictures of successes are especially effective. People are anxious to be seen as conforming to what the majority does.

4. Likability

We feel compelled to buy from people we like. People like each other because of similarity and attractiveness caused by dress, hairstyle, interests, origins, compliments, cooperation and courtesy. We find it difficult to resist a friend's request. We want to be identified with winners.

Our best defense against this weapon is to recognize when we are beginning to like the person selling to us more than we should. We should be especially wary of those who possess extraordinary charisma (they could sell an ice chest to an Eskimo in a snowstorm!). When we notice this feeling, we will be tipped off that a tactic is being used to create that feeling. We need to mentally separate the product being sold from the person selling it.

How can we use this weapon in our business? I feel it is often used most by successful beginning farriers. When people say the reason they use a farrier is because they "like him," this weapon is working. (I hope it is in addition to the high quality work the person does, not as a substitute for it.) We can tell people we like them and show it by giving them gifts, and sending cards and thank you notes at appropriate times. Frequent praise and compliments increase the intensity of a liking relationship. Association with the "rich and famous" also helps. Aligning ourselves with our clients on issues important to them is valuable. We need to avoid offending the client by our habits or comments.

5. Authority

We feel compelled to give obedience to authority. We will obey the commands of authority figures without thinking of the consequences. Religious and parental training contribute to this. Con artists use clothes, uniforms, positions, titles, size (they even wear shoe lifts and padding to make them taller and bigger) to get a favorable response. Things that are important to us seem bigger.

Our best defense against this weapon is to be more aware of the power of authority. We should ask ourselves: Is this authority an expert? And if so, how truthful can we expect the "expert" to be? In other words, to be believed competent and followed, a person must have both skill and character. Power comes with authority – and power is frequently abused.

How can we use this weapon in our business? Establish ourselves as authorities using credentials. If you choose to do this, you must educate people as to what it means. This might mean showing criteria or pictures of the exam and your certificate. Association with authorities in clinics or seminars, published articles you have written, and competition titles you have won will help establish your position. The connotation of authority can help.

6. Scarcity

We feel compelled to buy things that will be rare or unavailable later. We have a weakness for shortcuts. We feel that when an item is scarce, our freedom of choice is limited and we naturally rebel. Things that normally would have little appeal become more attractive when they are not now or soon will become unavailable. We are afraid we are going to miss something or lose something.

Our best defense against this weapon is to recognize the appeal to what we will lose instead of the benefits and genuine need for the product. We must recognize the pressure when it is applied before our logic is taken over by emotion. Scarce things are not any more useable than those that appear scarce. Competition is increased when rivalry is involved.

How can we use this weapon? This weapon has the least application in the horseshoeing business unless you apply it to yourself. Are you so popular and busy that it is difficult to get an appointment with you? This scarcity can be created to some extent by creative scheduling. Another is by positioning yourself as a unique and "rare" professional. Usually, people who use this weapon want to keep prospects from thinking by scaring them into wanting what they are selling now. This applies less to our services than it does to most products.

Marketing by Branding

Marketing is what one does to cause the public to want and buy your product or service. Marketing a business has become very complex. Marketing can be reduced to building a brand in the mind of the prospect. Today most products and services are bought, not sold. Marketers use branding to "pre-sell" the product or service to the user, a form of differentiation. Branding on the ranch differentiates your cow from other cattle on the range, even though cattle all look pretty much alike.

Try to apply this to your business. As in the cattle world, a branded product or service is easier to sell than a maverick. The application of the techniques used by major product and service companies to help position our businesses as unique and recognizable will also make us a "brand" name.

For a detailed explanation of these techniques, see *The 22 Immutable Laws of Branding* by Al and Laura Ries, published by Harper Business Books.

Chapter 11

How to Build a Customer Base for Your Business

Chapter 11

How to Build a Customer Base for Your Business

Building Value in the Mind of the Customer

Ask most beginning farriers how to build a customer base and they will say to increase volume, shoe more horses. But there are many other ways to build a better base; volume is only one of them. The most important way is to build value in the mind of the customer, then manage a database and build repeat business.

Convince people of your desire to be of service and to do the job right. Professionals sell value; amateurs sell price. People buy higher-priced things because they perceive more value. Marketing is helping people see value in what you have to sell that is greater than the price they must pay to get it. Market studies have shown that only 10% of customers make buying decisions based on price (or availability) alone. Customers in the other 90% base decisions on their perception of quality – which differs for each person. Therefore, the quality of your service must be communicated or sold to the client. This requires self-discipline and focused marketing.

Here are 10 powerful ways to build value in the minds of your customers.

1. Presentation

The way in which you present yourself can add or detract from the value in the customer's mind. This includes personal appearance, grooming, clothes, truck and tools. A piece of cake that has been colorfully decorated, carefully cut and beautifully served has more value than a piece of cake that is offered after it has been picked up and squished between someone's fingers.

2. Attitude

How much you care about the clients' animals and their business is expressed in the way you treat them and care for them. Learn their names. Record and review notes before each visit. Be kind to both horses and people. Remember, people don't care how much you know until they know how much you care.

3. Humane treatment

Stress a humane approach for the horse's care. A high percentage of Americans believe horses have rights. Differentiate between welfare and rights. Use common sense to promote humane care.

4. Dependability

When your clients can count on you to be there consistently on time, your value increases. Most clients are more concerned about their farriers arriving on time ready to work than about credentials or experience.

5. Teaching

You can add value in the minds of your customers by educating them on how to care for their horses. Carry copies of useful articles, charts, specimens, books and tapes, then discuss these educational materials with your clients.

6. Training

Training increases your value tremendously because it increases your confidence in yourself to do the job right. It probably doesn't matter to the client whether or not you have a particular certification. But it does matter that you have the confidence to know what to do in the situations in which their horses need your exper-

tise. Display certificates and discuss your continuing education experiences.

7. Successful Cases

You can show your client your ability to perform good work by creating and carrying with you a portfolio of your successful cases. Make it an excellent, professional presentation. Nothing succeeds like success.

8. Reputation

Value can be created through reputation. You *will* be talked about. What do you want people to say? You can enhance your visibility, name recognition and reputation by writing articles for local publications, sponsoring events and conducting programs. Avoid fads. It takes years to build a reputation and seconds to ruin it.

9. Consultation

Sell the client on the value of your consultation. Consulting should be part of the bill. Consulting is where the line is crossed between education and experience to practical application. Your understanding of what to do in a particular situation is of tremendous value to your clients since they do not have the experience or skill you have.

10. Gratitude

Thank people for their business. Send thank-you notes and gifts to clients who provide you with new business or referrals. A short note can go a long way in building the value of your service. Your best customers should receive more gratitude than your occasional customers.

Understanding the Client

Much of your success in the business will be due to the type of client you choose to align yourself with. Some of this is due to natural attraction based on similar interests. More is due to your ability to "read" and understand the client's situation.

Dr. Robert Miller wrote an article in the Nov/Dec 1989 issue of *Equine Veterinary Science* that can help you understand the client's motivation. Here are some highlights.

- Most of America's horses are companion animals. Even most working animals, which amount to less than one-tenth of our equine population, have an emotional bond with their masters. It is important to identify and understand the animal's role in the client's life, because horses are kept for very diverse reasons. The horse may serve the role of surrogate child. It may be a surrogate friend, mate, slave or even master. Sometimes the identification with the animal is so strong, it tends to look like and behave like the owner.

- The horse may be used to seek attention or to display the client's inner self in the horse habit. Or he may use the horse to promote an admired image.

- People will often say they keep horses because they love them, but you question this when you learn they only like certain breeds or types. These people will ask you if you have horses to assure themselves that you, too, love horses. True horsemen love all types and all disciplines. However, horse people can be quite incompatible with each other; they have a hard time agreeing on anything.

- Some owners keep a horse because it is a reminder of the value of work. These owners like a challenge and enjoy seeing the result of their training efforts in a working horse.

- The horse may be important to people because it moves them around and physically manipulates their bodies. They feel better while moving.

- The horse can help the client play a role of cowboy, frontiersman, soldier or wealthy sophisticate. The client can participate in fantasy without the danger and hardship associated with it.

- The horse may be a means of beating others, of winning competitions. These owners are often aggressive with a single goal of winning.

- The horse may be chosen because of its ability to make a weak and inexperienced rider look like an expert due to its calm nature and smooth gaits.

Why are so many horses owned by women? Women are probably less intimidating to a timid and lazy creature like the horse. Women tend to use their minds rather than their muscles to train horses. I believe there is an ex-

> *The European influence on horsemanship in America has brought an element of art that tends to replace utility.*

change of emotion that is not as common with male handlers. Women tend to be more nurturing than men. Horses can probably sense this. Some women like horses because of the feeling of mastery of such a large and powerful animal, and the freedom they feel when riding.

The European influence on horsemanship in America has brought an element of art that tends to replace utility. The rapport that can exist between horse and rider is very appealing, especially to older, single women. But some horses are kept only to be viewed as art objects.

Since people and their reasons for keeping horses are so varied, it requires some effort and sensitivity to identify with clients' needs, especially when their values and motivations are different from your own.

Building Client Relationships

Here are seven guidelines for establishing and maintaining a good relationship with the clients for whom you work.

1. **Make a good first impression.**

   It is easier to build a good long-term relationship with a client when the first impression is favorable. You only have one chance to make a good first impression. People make impressions by phone, prompt arrival, personal presentation – dress, grooming, appearance, smell (carry clean clothes, wash up in a bucket)], manners and courtesy – by advertising, billing and appreciation for business. If you wish to be successful, you must advertise success. Is your first impression working for you?

2. Build value in the mind of the customer.

Convince people of your desire to be of service and to do it right. Show them you are providing excellent service because of your training, experience and credentials. As was previously mentioned, your attitude, training and dependability have tremendous value. If they have a pleasant experience with you, the good feeling they have will cause them to value your work over your competitors. Helping people feel good has value.

3. Devote time and attention to strong clients; ignore the weak ones.

You need to have a system for identifying and prioritizing strong clients for your business. Vilfredo Pareto, an Italian marketing specialist, developed the rule that 20% of your clients will give you 80% of your business. That means focusing your time on giving great service to fewer clients (the same few), and not new ones all of the time. Write notes, leave messages, give gifts that reinforce your relationship. Offer to present programs for clubs.

4. Show empathy for the concerns of your clients.

Create a systematic way to record and remember the specific names of horses you work with. These records should include both problems and successes you have had in shoeing their horses. More horse owners are keeping their horses for longer periods of time. Ask your clients about their feelings toward their horses and note their responses. Try to understand the client's needs, not yours. To show concern for them, give gifts of articles, booklets and tapes.

5. Set up standards for hours and appointments.

Determine when you will begin your work and when you will end it for the day and week. Tell your clients you will not shoe before a certain time of day or after a certain time. Make sure to schedule your appointments around vacations and your days off. Schedule your next appointment after you have completed your work. Write the new appointment on the bill. Do this scheduling as a convenience for the client. You might even consider charging clients more if they book the appointment later. Let your appointment secretary remind clients or reschedule their appointments. Try to group client appointments geographically. A lack of planning on the client's part does not constitute an emergency on your part! Reschedule a special time for "lost" shoe replacement. Get good directions from your first-time clients and repeat them back. Then remember to record them in your phone directory or database. Finally, be sure you are on time for your appointments. If you can't be on time, call by cellular or pay phone to let them know. However, make sure your cellular phone doesn't invite danger. A 1997 Canadian study showed that people talking on a cell phone when driving were four times more likely to be involved in an accident.

6. **Set up standards for your terms of payment.**

   Payment is due when your work or the service is completed. Control how the fees for your services are received. If you don't set up a standard procedure and stick to it, your clients will control how and when you receive compensation for your services.

7. **Emphasize the benefits of using your services.**

   After listing the services you offer, emphasize the benefits of hiring you over your competition. Then support your claims with credentials and testimonials.

   For example, we offer the following services:

   a. *TRIMMING AND SHOEING*

      - *All breeds, all types*
      - *Therapeutic shoeing*
      - *Show horse shoeing*

   b. *SHOE MAKING*

      - *Specialty shoes*
      - *Therapeutic shoes*
      - *Hospital treatment plates*

c. *CONSULTING*

- *Soundness evaluation*

- *Conformation assessment*

- *Complete horse and rider evaluation*

d. *ADVANCED FARRIER TRAINING*

- *One-On-One*

- *Small Group Work shops*

- *Large Group Seminars*

These are the ways our services will benefit you and your horse(s):

1. *You will achieve effective and long-term results with customized shoeing focused on your horse's challenges.*

2. *You will learn effectively and efficiently with interactive teaching and consulting designed to eliminate the guesswork from what you do.*

3. *You will stay on the cutting edge with what is happening in the industry.*

4. *You will get answers to your highly specific questions based on experience, not speculation.*

5. *You will save time and money by making better decisions and having fewer problems.*

6. *You will increase your powers of observation and assessment as you learn to "see" so you can "find" hidden solutions to your horse's challenges.*

7. *You will have a more rewarding experience with your horse as you learn how to meet its needs from its perspective, not yours.*

Setting Fees with Clients

Keep in mind these 10 principles when working with your clients and considering a fair price to be paid for your services.

1. Charge all clients the same. If you offer special rates to certain customers, you will eventually end up having to cut prices for others as well. Price cutting is a self-inflicted wound. Set your price and let your clients make the decision.

2. Stress the value of your work in fulfilling the client's objectives. Use formulas for time and hours worked until you can establish value.

3. Consulting should be part of the bill after the client is sold on your value.

4. Your travel time is billable time. Make circles around your base. Charge by the minute rather than the mile. Mountains and dirt roads

slow you down, after all, and time is money.

5. Convey enthusiasm. ("I Am Sold Myself.") Clients purchase you, not just the job. Enthusiasm and energy can be generated by repeating positive affirmations each day, such as, "I am good. I do good work. I provide good service. I care about these people. I deserve these rates."

6. Stress your experience, training and credentials. Attitude, dependability and training have tremendous value.

7. Don't allow yourself to make a differentiation in quality of work between clients. If you do, it won't be long before you won't be able to remember the difference. Do your best work every time.

8. Focus on what you do well – your specialty. If more advanced work needs to be done, refer that work to other specialists. Be competency-level conscious. You should be charging at your level. If you are only capable of doing work at a lower level, you shouldn't be charging the price that a more advanced farrier would charge. If, on the other hand, you are a high-level farrier and aren't

charging what you are worth, you are hurting yourself.

9. Regularly turn down 10% of the work that comes your way. This may include those you presently serve or those who are new, potential clients. This practice gives you time to give exceptional service to those clients who appreciate and value your work.

10. Only change your base rate when clients provide important concessions that justify it – if they bring the horse to you or allow a helper to work on it, for example.

The Value of Integrity

People value integrity. When my brother went to work for the local bank, my father said, "Remember, all you have to sell is your integrity." That is all any of us have to sell. Since it is so highly valued, we must structure our business affairs to deliver integrity every time. The following story illustrates the power of integrity.

Richard Jackson was a farmer who was arrested during the Revolutionary War and charged with planning to join the King's forces. He was too honest to deny his intentions, so he was turned over to the sheriff, and committed to the county jail. He could have easily escaped from the jail, but honesty was so much a part of his life that he prepared himself to receive the consequences. After having been in jail for a few days, he asked the jailer to let him go out during the day to work, promising he would return by nightfall. His integrity was so well known that he was immediately given permission. For eight months, Jackson went out every day to work and came back to jail faithfully at night. In May, the sheriff prepared to take him to Springfield, where he would be tried for treason. Jackson told the sheriff that he could save himself the trouble and expense as Jackson could go by himself. The sheriff allowed this, and Jackson set off for Springfield. On the way, he was met in the woods by a Mr. Edwards, a member of the Council of Massachusetts, which at that time was the supreme executive body of the state. Mr. Edwards asked Mr. Jackson where he was going. "To Springfield, sir, to be tried for my life."

In Springfield, Richard Jackson was found guilty and condemned to death. He immediately appealed to the Council for mercy. The evidence was presented to the Council and the President put the question before the council of whether the pardon should be granted. He said the case was perfectly clear. The act was unquestionably high treason, and the proof was complete, and if mercy was shown in this case, he saw no reason why it should not be granted in every other case. One by one the members of the Council agreed with the President, until it came time for Mr. Edwards to speak. He was the man whom Mr. Jackson had met in the woods. Instead of delivering his opinion, he simply related the whole story of meeting Jackson in the woods. The Council was so moved by Jackson's integrity, its members decided that such a man certainly should not be sent to the gallows. So Jackson was pardoned. Integrity sells.

Once, I took a travel trailer I owned into a dealership in a Western state to see what I could sell it for. The owner offered me a fair price, but said he had to pay me by check. I was concerned if the check would be good, as I was a visitor to that town and didn't know the man. I went to the local bank before making the deal and asked the first available teller, "What can you tell me about this man?" She said, "Sir, whatever that man gives you will be as good as gold." I was impressed. I went back and told the man what the teller said, and he got teary-eyed when he realized the effect of his reputation. That sort of integrity is something we should all strive for. It can be a great help in building and sustaining our customer base.

Professional Ethics

A survey was taken of 235 horse owners at Purina Equine Education Seminars in 1999. They rated people in the following order for professionalism in ethics. You might say this is the "pecking order" of the horse industry. This survey helps us understand how farriers are perceived by the horse-owning public. The numbers represent the percentage of horse owners who thought the named group showed positive professionalism or ethics.

The argument that education increases the ethics and professionalism of a person is obviously untrue. People feel that the attitudes and image of those who practice in the various "professions" is more important than the years of education they receive. Much of ethics perception is based on our personal experience in relationships during our lives. For example, extension agents may be perceived as bureaucratic rather than trained professionals because they are part of government. The position of these professional groups is probably determined by their authority status. The characteristic of authority has been shown to count heavily in product and service selection.

People Skills

Dale Carnegie's book *How to Win Friends and Influence People* is one of the most important books you can read and study to help build your customer base, be more effective in your work, and become successful in the farrier business. It is one of the best-selling books of all time. Taking the Dale Carnegie Course is a good investment and will help you in many ways to grow as a person, and, in turn, grow your business. Many years ago, I signed up everyone in my family who was old enough to take the course.

The basic premise of the book is summed up in principles or rules to live by. These should be memorized and reviewed regu-

Those showing positive professionalism:	Those showing positive ethics:
88.5 veterinarians	78.3 veterinarians
79.5 physicians	68.8 physicians
78.3 dentists	61.3 dentists
66.0 horse trainers	57.8 farriers
62.6 farriers	56.2 horse trainers
57.0 attorneys	54.5 horse extension specialists

Source: American Farriers Journal, Mar/Apr 1999, p.7.

larly, so they will be applied daily. I encourage you to find a Dale Carnegie Course in your area. It will tremendously improve your ability to work well with people. Other timeless subjects are covered by Dale Carnegie in the book *How to Win Friends and Influence People*, with special emphasis on how to give and receive criticism. We need to encourage others for every improvement, let them save face, and give them a fine reputation to live up to. Use praise instead of criticism when dealing with people. Both horses and people respond better and learn faster when criticism is minimized and praise is emphasized. Reinforce the good behavior, and the bad behavior will be starved for lack of attention.

The principles taught by Mr. Carnegie will only work if they come from the heart. We must change the way we think, if we want to be effective.

Changing How We Think

Dr. Stephen Covey, in his book *The Seven Habits of Highly Effective People*, quoted Anwar Sadat, the great Egyptian leader who worked to improve the relations between the Arabs and Israelis. Sadat's statement was: "It was then that I drew, almost unconsciously, on the inner strength I had developed, . . . call it a talent or capacity, for change. I found

that I faced a highly complex situation, and that I couldn't hope to change it until I had armed myself with the necessary psychological and intellectual capacity. My contemplation of life and human nature . . . had taught me that he who cannot change the very fabric of his thought will never be able to change reality, and will never, therefore, make any progress."

We can change the world around us, but we must recognize that real change only comes from inside. It doesn't come by trying to manipulate others, but rather from changing the very fabric of our thought. As we do this, our character changes, we view the world differently, and our business changes as we change ourselves.

William James, one of America's most distinguished psychologists, said, "Compared with what we ought to be, we are only half awake. We are making use of only a small part of our physical and mental resources. Stating the thing broadly, the human individual thus lives far within his limits. He possesses powers of various sorts which he habitually fails to use."

Business Advice for Beginners

Perhaps my advice to beginners is best summarized in the answers I gave to questions asked by the managing editor of the *American Farriers Journal*.

1. **What three business tips would you give graduating farriers that would make them the most profit in the first year?**

I would recommend graduating farriers *not* be concerned about how much profit they will earn in the first year. Rather, they should be concerned about how much they can *learn*. This may mean being an apprentice to an established, highly skilled farrier, and accepting challenges that are at or above his or her ability. Ask for critique and expert supervision. Daily forging practice, even after a hard day's work, is necessary in making progress as a farrier at this time. It takes years to become competent at farrier skills. The learning curve can be shortened by focused practice.

2. **What are the biggest shoeing and business mistakes farriers make in the first year after graduating?**

The biggest mistake farriers make is going to work on their own without being skilled enough to handle all of the situations they will encounter. Mistakes are vividly remembered for a long time by clients and may hamper future business growth. Don't put yourself in a position to be embarrassed. Don't argue with clients. Work on improving your people skills as well as your shoeing skills. Word travels fast. Work with others until you feel competent to go on your own. Be honest with yourself as well as your clients. Refer work that is above your level of expertise.

3. **What business and shoeing advice would you give farriers who have been shoeing for five years?**

Farriers who have been shoeing for five years should continue to grow in skill and efficiency, skills should be practiced and applied to everyday work. Clients should be treated as valuable business partners.

You can hold on to those you have by providing superior service and don't expand until you have a solid client base. Weed out those with whom you feel uncomfortable for one reason or another, and provide extraordinary service for those who meet your criteria as superior clients or "A" customers.

John Kador's article "Common Mistakes by Young Business Persons" from *Home Office Computing*, Sept 1996, gives us some directions about handling mistakes. His points follow.

Common Mistakes by Young Business Persons

1. They underestimate their own influence.

If it is to be, it's up to me. You are the business. Search for systems.

2. They compromise their principles/values to get or keep business.

Trust your feelings and the reality that you can't work with everybody.

3. They hire a critical employee without necessary experience.

If you are too busy to train, don't deny your feelings and impressions.

4. They don't choose clients wisely.

Best to choose on the basis of stability and reputation, not appearance. Even if they pay slower, they are better in the long run.

5. They don't continue to market to their good accounts.

Avoid overconfidence and overwork, as they blind you to reality.

6. They insist on doing everything themselves.

Hire experts to help you with specialized needs – seek professional advice.

7. They forget to insure against unforeseen catastrophes.

Obtain health, life and liability insurance that protects you from exposure.

8. They fall behind in new technology and techniques.

Take time to master the basics. Keep up.

Networking Skills

A very underused tool by farriers and other horse professionals, networking is the process of making connections with other people for mutually beneficial exchange of ideas, information and contacts. Become known as the person who has the answer or can help find it.

People skills account for 85% of a person's success on the job; whereas, technical skills only account for 15%. Networking is one of the most useful of the people skills.

Business educator Peter Drucker was quoted in the November 1997 issue of *AFJ* (page 10) as saying that we only have a 1 in 16 chance to sell to a person we don't know, a 1 in 4 chance to sell to an inactive customer (one whom we have done business with before) and a 1 in 2 chance to sell more products and services to an active customer.

Networking can be fun as well as productive. Set goals to place yourself in networking situations several times a week. Set your goals backward. If you want a new client, you may have to contact 10 people, four of whom will be interested and one of them will become a new client. Never say you are busy when someone asks how business is. Instead, say, "Business is great, but I'm looking for more! Do you know of any?"

The average person knows 250 people, according to Bob Burg, author of *Endless Referrals*, published by McGraw-Hill. That means to glean referrals, you need to begin to tap every potential source you encounter.

Paying for referrals with discounts or gifts is called "bird-dogging" in the car business, according to Joe Girard in his book *How to Sell Anything to Anybody*. Joe says, "People don't buy a product, they buy me (or you). I can tell it in their eyes."

Bird-dogging refers to hunting (for prospects) with bird dogs. It works in any industry. The important thing is to pay or reward someone for hunting for you. These rewards can be in the form of payments, discounts on service or products, or certificates for food or merchandise.

Ask questions about the other person's life, needs and feelings. Avoid talking about yourself.

When you listen, they will think you are much more interesting than if you tell them all about yourself. Most people listen to only one radio station, WIIFM (What's In It For Me). Don't cause them to tune you out by talking about inappropriate things.

You can analyze your opportunities to network by categorizing the areas where you come in contact with people in your life. You will probably have seven or eight areas, such as church, school, associations, clubs, fitness, family, friends, co-workers, neighbors, health professionals and clients. Set a goal to meet one or more people in each of these areas each day or each week.

Use your business cards to put your name and contact information in other people's databases and be sure to get theirs or the appropriate information for your database.

Your database can be a computer program, called a Contact Management System, a Rolodex, a 3x5 card file or a phone directory in your day planner. There are a few systems designed especially for farriers. *Clincher* is one of the oldest. *Forge Ahead* is one of the newest. *Farrier Basic* is very popular. Other programs such as *Access*, *Act!* and *Equine Data Management* can be adapted to your business. The important thing is to file a person's name where it is retrievable, make notes to aid memory and periodically contact the person.

Follow-up your meeting(s) with a note to keep in personal contact. This keeps you in people's minds so they will remember you at the time when they need a service or are asked for a referral. Always acknowledge and reward referral business.

When talking on the phone, always answer with energy and enthusiasm. It is all right to be a little phony if you don't feel well. (Most of the work in the world is done by people who don't feel very well.) The phone is often the first face of your business that people "see."

In summary, find common ground to start with and look for ways to share information. Ask questions about people and follow up by networking with others in mutually beneficial ways to share the products and services you sell.

How to Obtain Great Referrals

Here are seven powerful ways to increase the quantity and quality of business contacts and referrals.

1. Build your reputation. Do good work. Run a professional business. You will be talked about. Learn everything you can about farriery. Ben Franklin said, "If a man empties his purse into his head, no

man can take it away from him." An investment in knowledge always pays the best dividends. Write articles for local newspapers, journals, etc., to give yourself credibility and exposure. Provide exceptional service and demonstrate integrity while you are with clients. Always be on time and strive to add value to everything you do. Educate clients and give them gifts. If you consistently provide exceptional service, clients will provide you with excellent referrals when asked.

2. Create a program to offer to 4-H, Pony Clubs, Expos, Horse Clubs. If you present an excellent professional presentation, horse owners will talk about you and refer you to their friends. Seek opportunities to share your program with groups of horseowners.

3. Refer business you are not comfortable with to upper or lower level farriers. Collect business cards. Refer to them and expect them to refer to you. This is done in other professions, why not ours? Here

is how this can work: An inexperienced farrier just out of school obtains a client with a barn full of horses, but there is one horse that is laminitic. He or she knows that if they start working on that horse, they are in over their heads. So, instead of doing it, they could say to the owner, "I think you need to have a more experienced farrier come in and do this horse. I am a 'general practitioner' horseshoer, and therefore, I am recommending that you have a 'specialist' farrier work on this problem horse. This farrier will charge more than I do because he/she has a lot more experience and more training. It takes longer to do this specialized job." Then they can expect that farrier to refer work to them that is not as technical. I do this with several farriers in my area, and they like it. They know I will charge their clients two or three times what they charge to do regular shoeing. So, the owners don't want me for their regular shoeing, but the beginning farrier also knows he/she is out from under the problems of a complicated job. It then becomes my problem, and I am going to do the very best I can to solve it. I am not a threat to take over the other horses in that barn. Instead, I am a complement to the beginning farrier's business.

4. Send thank you notes and gifts to those who give you referrals. A referral is a powerful vote of confidence. Show your gratitude. Experts recommend at least 5% of your profit be given to those who give referrals.

5. Build relationships with other equine professionals.

   a. Trainers – Generally, trainers will know the horses you work on much better than you do. Ask for their advice. They are also networked with many other trainers and horse professionals to whom they will refer your services if you earn their trust.

   b. Veterinarians – The relationship between the farrier and the veterinarian is at best a blessing and at worst a nightmare. Here are guidelines for establishing a good relationship with veterinarians.

1) Recognize that you are both in the customer service business. Consider the client's concerns and provide for the needs and long-term welfare of the horse.

2) Recognize that each of you has strengths. The farrier typically has more experience with foot problems and horsemanship skills. The veterinarian usually has more education in physiology and pathology. The farrier knows about current foot products. The veterinarian knows drugs that are useful for behavior, infection and pain control.

3) Recognize that each of you has limitations and concerns or fears. Farriers fear intimidation by formally educated people and lack of respect for their experiences. Vets fear they will miss the problem while looking for all of the possibilities. They also are concerned about lack of respect for their expensive education.

4) Recognize how the owner views each of you and the problem at hand. The typical barn pecking order is perceived as trainer, vet, farrier, farm help. The owner may view his or her animals as family members and be emotionally involved in their care. To the owner, how you treat the animals may be more important than your procedure or technique.

5) Recognize good barn help. They know the horses and can protect you and make your experience more pleasant if they like you.

6) Recognize how we all must work together. Remember, the best solution is one that values the differences between the farrier and the vet, yet produces synergy. Both must be free and comfortable doing his or her specific thing well, and agree before proceeding just what those areas are. Recommend each other to strengthen the client's confidence in each of you. Refer (or defer) to one another when it is appropriate. Recognize that the result of synergy is something better than either of you could have produced on your own. Realize you cannot work with everyone.

7) Respect each other's abilities and talents and expect professional respect in return. Don't let the owner use the farrier as an inexpensive vet!

8) Ask your current clients for referrals. Each of your clients should be treated as a very valuable resource for referrals. If they are sold on your value, they are usually happy to recommend you if asked. Give them gifts or thank-you notes for referring you to their friends or associates. A discount on the next shoeing job is one type of gift that is always appreciated. People like to give referrals.

9) Ask your suppliers to refer you for specific types of work. Get yourself in the data bases of related businesses so they can help their customers by referring you to them.

What Leaders Do To Be Effective

Leaders are effective. They spend time on producing results that pay off, not just on activity. They are role models. They become students of client behavior. Only human assets appreciate in value. The value of your business increases as your relationship with your clients improves. Make decisions with your brain, apply them with your heart.

Leaders work *on* their businesses, not just *in* them. They do the following to get to and stay in front.

1. Focus on customer satisfaction.

2. Analyze profit potential of each activity.

3. Emphasize product quality and service.

4. Build up people – customers and employees.

5. Develop an organization with systems.

6. Seek innovation to change what isn't working.

Lifetime Value of a Customer

It is important to know the lifetime value of a customer. How long has your average customer been with you? Your best "A" customers have great value to you. Calculating how much these people spend with you will help you appreciate their value to you. You will feel good about giving them extra service and even regular gifts when you realize how valuable they are to you.

Business-Building Enemies

Your worst enemy in business can be the "out-of-sight, out-of-mind" syndrome, according to Jim Rhode in *Marketing for People Not in Marketing*. To overcome this and to get people to buy from you repeatedly, you must figure out a way to overcome this problem. Ideally, repeat business accounts for 60% of your business and 80% of your profits.

One way to get your name in front of people is to send a mailing to your customers during the year. Even once a year is good. One successful New York farrier includes his policies, personal news, helpful hints and season's greetings in his annual newsletter.

Another way is to send birthday or holiday cards to remind people you care about them. Yet another way is to send a useful tool that they will see frequently. Examples include a hoof pick imprinted with your name, a calendar with your name, a sticker or magnet to go on the phone or refrigerator with a space for emergency phone numbers and your number as the farrier. Posters, coffee mugs, T-shirts, hats and buttons all keep your name in front of clients so they will think to recommend you.

Another enemy is spreading negative stories. According to Jerry R. Wilson, author of *Word of Mouth Marketing*, for every three people willing to tell a positive story, 33 will tell a negative story about your business. This is human nature. You must be good at what you do – but you must help people feel good about it, also. Tell them they did the right thing by hiring you to do their work. Praise their desires to do right by their horse(s). Think through a strategy to diffuse negative comments. Have a ready answer for the most commonly asked questions.

Why Clients Fire Farriers

Here is a list of reasons given by owners for changing farriers.

1. Failure to keep appointments.

2. Discourteous to client, family, friends.

3. Incompatible personalities.

4. Disciplined horse harshly.

5. Drinking or using tobacco on the job.

6. Horse becomes lame – attributed to farrier.

7. Criticism by respected friend or professional trainer, veterinarian, therapist or merchant.

8. Hard to contact – failure to return calls in a timely manner.

9. Not available for emergencies.

10. Not perceived to be skilled.

11. Not knowledgeable about industry/trade.

12. Incomplete inventory.

13. Too many add-ons.

14. Priced too high.

Why Farriers Fire Clients

You cannot and should not work with everyone. Here is a list of reasons given by farriers and veterinarians for dropping clients. The client:

1. Shows lack of courtesy and respect for your time, safety, comfort or skill.

2. Does not honor appointments.

3. Does not pay when service is rendered or in an agreed upon and timely manner.

4. Puts off payment due to financial irresponsibility.

5. Loses temper easily and takes it out on horseshoer, vet, horses, children or other clients.

6. Expects special treatment that takes attention from other clients.

7. Pits you against other farriers, veterinarians or horse professionals.

8. Will not follow through or follow directions for agreed-upon treatment.

9. Complains about your skill and service to you and others.

10. Makes threats of legal action against you or others.

11. Brags about taking advantage of others in business.

12. Complains (whines) about prices or business policies.

13. Refers other difficult clients to you.

14. Keeping them causes you financial, family or personal distress.

Chapter 12

How to Expand the Product and Service Base for Your Business

Chapter 12

How to Expand the Product and Service Base for Your Business

Sources of Income

Traditionally, farriers thought of themselves as skilled laborers or craftsmen. Many seemed to feel that was all they should ever be. Some even believed it was somehow wrong to be a merchant and sell anything other than their "backs." After all, there are only two professions that sell their bodies, and farriery is one of them!

On the other hand, many successful farriers today recognize the need to develop another source of income to support themselves when they no longer can or want to shoe horses. Many farrier suppliers and farrier equipment manufacturers started their businesses for this reason. The supply or manufacturing business that at first was part-time later became their full-time means of support.

The goal of all these activities is to develop a source or sources of residual income, which is money that comes to you without using your back. Jim Cathcart, in his book *The Acorn Principle,* calls this SWISS money (Sales While I Sleep Soundly).

Product Sales

Another option that most farriers have not fully explored is selling horse care products from their trucks directly to horse owners. Surveys show that horse owners trust their farriers' advice on feeding and caring for their horses. Farriers can make these repeat sales and build their source of income while providing a service to their clients. For example, selling nutritional supplements, such as Farriers Formula, can become a profitable residual income-producer. Farriers can handle other rapidly used-up products, such as thrush medications, horse treats, hoof dressings, liniments, shampoos, lead ropes and hoof picks.

Residual income continues to flow to you after you make the first sale or do the work. Sometimes, this is in the form of royalties or licenses to use your ideas or products sold after you make the first sale of a consumable product and clients look to you to continue supplying them.

Endorsements

Endorsements of products and sponsorships can provide additional income, depending on the contract. Endorsements are becoming popular in our industry, as can be seen from ads in farrier publications.

Before you choose to become a spokesman for a company, consider the implications. You will be linked to that company in the future and regarded as its representative and marketer. Your actions will reflect on the company. Conversely, its actions will reflect on you. Your credibility may be questioned, as you will be seen as a "promoter and salesman." The price of celebrity status may be more than you want to pay, unless you are completely sold on the company's product and business ethics. An initial friendship may not be enough to sustain a long-term relationship; get all agreements in writing.

Commission Selling

Farriers can arrange to sell all sorts of horse-related products while they visit with a client on the job. As an example, catalog sales are possible for tack of all types, non-prescription medicines, supplements, feeders, fencing and farm equipment. Or you can go to local distributors and set up an individual arrangement to sell products for them. All businesses want exposure to targeted customers. You can convince them your activities can benefit them. If you have one type of a client's business, it is easier to get more businesses from that same customer who likes and trusts you than it is to go out and find another customer. Jim Rhode, a marketing strategist writing in *Marketing for People Not in Marketing*, says that repeat business should account for at least 60% of your business and 80% of your profits.

Think about all the things horse owners buy. A partial list might include hay, buckets, grain, feeders, fencing, arena jumps, rails, ropes, saddles, other tack, jewelry, saddle pads, halters, brushes, farm equipment, lumber, posts, farm tools, books, tapes and magazines. How could you serve your present clients by helping them get these items and, at the same time, build another income source for yourself?

National Referral Data Bases

Membership in some organizations makes you part of their databases. These lists are frequently shared and can be a means of expanding your exposure to potential customers. This is especially true of state farrier associations. When they get calls requesting a farrier in your area, they will give your name and contact information, if it is available. You can use these lists also to serve your customers when they move by putting them in touch with a qualified farrier in their new location. If you don't know the individuals listed, it is best to give several names so the client makes the choice, not you – especially since competency standards are not universally recognized.

Veterinary Liaison

You can also expand your service base by creating a liaison, or relationship, with one or more of the veterinarians who serve your area. If you do it right and work with veterinarians you respect, then they, in turn, respect you and you both will prosper. Recognize that veterinarians can help or hurt you. An effective, lasting liaison comes from mutual understanding as well as respect.

1. Historical Origin

Traditionally, the veterinarian/ farrier relationship has been adversarial; farriers and veterinarians just didn't like each other. The veterinary profession actually evolved from the farrier profession. In fact, before 1800, they were one and the same. Then they began to separate on the continent of Europe. The farriers or blacksmith/horseshoers took the path of least resistance, much to their discredit, becoming known as the ignorant, the lax, the leeches, the quacks and every other terrible name that could be thought of. The veterinarians, on the other hand, chose the path of education and growth. They established schools and developed training programs. Most of them were short-term, what we would today call a trade school. None of the early schools required more than a few months of classes, much like our American farrier schools today. However, they improved and progressed until professional schools, requiring several years of study, were established. Veterinarians called themselves veterinary surgeons in the British Isles to distinguish themselves from farriers.

2. Economic Competition

The second key to understanding veterinary/farrier relationships is economic. Veterinarians and farriers see themselves in competition for the same person's dollar. Actually, this is rarely true, but it is a widespread perception just the same. Veterinarians who shoe horses and farriers who float teeth don't help this situation at all. State practice acts are written to prevent what should be common sense. Such foolish indiscretion destroys your positioning and potential for success. Regardless of the reason, many vets and farriers see each other as competitors rather than cooperators. They believe the horse owner will call either one or the other.

3. Half-Brain Thinking

The third reason (and perhaps the main one) for the animosity between vet and farrier stems from ignorance of major differences between people. Will Rogers used to say, "Everybody is ignorant, only on different subjects." A corollary is, everybody is good, only at different things. We need to understand our differences and work together, using our strengths to solve problems.

Veterinarians spend many years studying and being "emotionally beat-up the entire time they are in veterinary school," according to Loretta Guage in her book *If Wishes Were Horses*. They develop their left-brain capabilities to a very high degree. The left side of the brain houses logical, numerical and verbal skills.

Farriers, on the other hand, are usually not as schooled and disciplined as vets. They tend to be more right-brained, housing spatial, intuitive and visual skills. And they get physically beat-up by unruly horses.

People using different thinking modes usually don't communicate very well. They are speaking different languages; they are speaking "the language of the deaf," according to Steven Covey. Instead of working toward synergy,

> *We need to understand our differences and work together, using our strengths to solve problems.*

which gives a solution that is better than each could have arrived at separately, we frequently go ahead on our own and get a half-brained solution! The corollary is that we don't see the world as *it* is, but as *we* are.

4. Practical versus Scientific Approach

Farriers are primarily mechanical in their approach to problems. They develop their skill by repetition and feel. What they do has to be practical and make sense to them. Farriers want to immediately try what they think will work (because it worked on the last horse they tried it on). They have a tendency to be very sure of things they've learned by experience.

Veterinarians, on the other hand, are trained to use the scientific method to evaluate and prescribe a medical solution. They must go through a process of differential diagnosis to eliminate all the possibilities. This often takes time. They are taught to be cautious, use only tested and proven procedures, and be non-committal in phrasing answers. They rely on the word of "experts" to help them make up their minds.

Can you see how this different way of looking at a problem could cause conflict?

5. Self-Taught versus System-Taught

Farriers are largely self-taught, mainly because they have no ongoing formal training system to rely on in this country. This often produces narrowness and even blindness. As a rule, they are academically deficient in scientific training. Farriers may have great ability and be highly skilled, but have little understanding of medical physiology.

On the other hand, in today's veterinary educational system, graduates have little mechanical or practical experience. If they do have any, they obtained it before attending vet school. A former student wrote me on her first day at vet school, saying, "One of my professors said by way of introduction that today's veterinary medicine involves two distinct operations: acquisition of knowledge and acquisition of skills. You will leave school full of the former and all but devoid of the latter." This is not the graduate veterinarian's fault. It is the fault of the system we have allowed to be built into our American veterinary schools.

Those who have tried to change the system faced many hurdles, as noted in an excellent book on this subject. Written by Henry Collins, an Australian veterinary teacher, it's called *Shedding the Blinkers in Veterinary Education*, published in 1996 by the University of Sydney Post Graduate Foundation.

Even though some changes have been tried in America, they haven't helped much. For example, schools have experimented with tracking to provide a more focused curriculum, but students did poorly on Boards that were designed for a more general curriculum. The dean of a large American veterinary school was quoted by the media as saying, "Today's veterinary education is a mile wide and an inch deep." Clearly, the current systems need a major overhaul.

Vet students are up against ferocious competition in higher education. The emotional and physical abuse that students survive makes them qualified to "swim with the sharks," as author and businessman Harvey McKay says. Some *don't* survive, they even lose their families and their identities in this hostile environment. Those who do survive learn how to get along in an adversarial and critical environment.

Most farriers have not been required to deal with these emotionally toughening experiences. That may explain why they often have a hard time dealing with critical evaluation and differences of opinion that contribute to conflict.

6. Return on Investment

Little investment is required to become a farrier. Since there are no required exams, anyone can start in farrier work. A person simply needs to be willing to work hard and take the time to learn the basics over a period of a few months. One can get into business for an investment of a few thousand dollars for schooling and tools. The most variable expense is the truck setup used.

Few professions have such a low cost of entry compared with the kind of income possible. The biggest unknown is how long it takes to build a sustainable business. For many, it's between two to five years. Yet some farriers are able to earn as much as veterinary or law school graduates in a few years.

Many farrier students are so anxious to get out of school and start making money that they don't make the best use of their learning time. After school, they don't continue to learn because they don't have to. The public simply doesn't expect or demand it. In my experience, the biggest mark of difference among top farriers is their desire for continuing education.

Veterinarians, on the other hand, enter a job that offers a very low return on their investment of time and money. First, they must take a rigorous undergraduate science curriculum and achieve a high-grade point average. Because application to vet school is highly

Vet students are up against ferocious competition in higher education.

competitive, odds are great they don't get in the first time they apply. They must be committed and persistent. And they must have financial resources. Tuition for four years of vet school is an average of $100,000. The average debt a veterinary student carries is $60,000, and it often takes about 10 years to pay it off. By contrast, the beginning salary for vet graduates averages $30,000 to $35,000 per year.

I doubt most farriers understand how tough it is to become a vet and how little respect they get for the effort and sacrifice they make to get there. Few careers give such a low return on the investment required.

Over the years, I taught in various vet schools and met numerous students who were more motivated from the expectation of their parents than they were from internal sources. They thought they wanted to do something with animals, and their parents wanted them to get paid well. So they were often pushed into a profession they were not interested in. The job didn't really fit their ability and internal motivation. In reality, the parents wanted to be able to tell their friends their child was a "doctor" and had a "real" job.

Bruce Daniels, an expert harness racehorse farrier from New Jersey and author of *Sunday On The Farm*, used to say that his in-laws would often ask his wife, "When is Bruce going to quit shoeing horses and get a real job?" I guess a lot of people feel like farriers don't have a real job. They ask, "Why do they get paid so much for doing something so simple?" Most people have never tried it, and therefore cannot understand. Yet few jobs give such a high return on the investment required to enter the field. Not surprisingly, this difference between farriers and vets is a source of conflict.

> *In my experience, the biggest mark of difference among top farriers is their desire for continuing education.*

7. Regulation and Licensing

Veterinarians are highly regulated by governments, while farriers have little or no regulation. This can't help but cause jealousy and feelings of unfairness. Veterinarians have education and licensing requirements. They have a long list of things they can and cannot do. Because they are recognized as part of a profession, they can be held to specified standards of behavior and obtain professional liability insurance.

Yet since farriers don't have an educational or licensing system, they cannot be held to as high a standard of responsibility as veterinarians. They can say, "Oh, I'm just a farrier! You can't expect too much from me. I'm just a step above a common laborer." It is hard to make negligence stick if there is no required formal training and/or mandatory qualification exam.

Veterinary practice laws are different in each state. These really serve as protectionist legislation that prevents unqualified persons from practicing any form of veterinary medicine. Some states allow dentists to treat horses while others make it illegal to put a float in a horse's mouth without a vet license. Most veterinary practice laws include working on the foot. Only in a few states is horseshoeing officially exempt. Tradition is all that keeps farriers out of trouble. The best position for farriers is to avoid crossing the line by doing anything to treat sensitive tissue.

Recently, a number of suits have been filed against practitioners in the "alternative" or "complementary" therapy community. The result is usually that the veterinarian has authority in most cases. They then can refer a case to another "practitioner" if it will complement prescribed medical treatment. Of course, the client can make the choice initially not to include the veterinarian. This also creates bad feelings.

8. Public Perception

How does the public perceive the expertise of farriers versus veterinarians? This survey reported in the Mar/Apr 2000 of *AFJ* gives us important clues.

Who would you call *first* if your horse had these problems?

	Farrier	Vet
Hoof crack	88.5%	11.5%
Sand crack	86.0%	14.0%
Thrush	71.2%	28.8%
Hoof bruise	70.3%	29.7%
Hoof abscess	41.7%	58.3%
Hoof wound	37.4%	62.6%
Laminitis/founder	20.5%	79.5%
Navicular	19.3%	80.7%

Survey by *AFJ* of 2,100 *Equus* readers/horse owners (11% response).

There has been a tremendous shift in how the majority of the people view animals. Historically and legally, animals have been regarded as property. People have made decisions regarding an animal's care based on its economic value. Not today. Animals are thought to have "rights" by the majority of people. Most animal care decisions are based on emotion, not common-sense logic.

Believing an animal has rights is different than believing in animal welfare. We all should be champions of, and believe in, promoting animal welfare. Animal welfare means taking good care of animals and looking after their needs from their point of view. Humane health, nutrition, environment and foot maintenance come under this category.

Animal rights means animals are equal to, or more valuable than, humans and deserve the same rights as humans do. The most radical of these groups believe that animals should not be "exploited" by being ridden, worked against their will, kept in enclosures or slaughtered for food. It is a position no responsible farrier or veterinarian can take.

The *Journal of Animal Science* did a survey of incoming freshmen in the Animal Science major across the United States in the early 1990s. Researchers found that 80% of these young people believed that animals had rights. A major Western horse magazine reported that 95% of their readers declared they believed in animal rights. Clearly, public perception is changing. Farriers and veterinarians need to be aware of this and be seen as a source for sensible solutions involving animal welfare.

9. Respect, Trust and Courtesy

Most farriers and veterinarians feel they don't get enough respect. Respect and trust must be earned. When we try to obtain these values through intimidation or titles, it isn't genuine. Now that we understand each other's origins and difficulties, perhaps it is time to share this story.

I once read Art Linkletter's autobiography. In it, he told the story of his first meeting with Henry J. Kaiser. Kaiser developed and manufactured several automobiles, had a number of patents and developed one of the first health care plans. Everyone called Henry Kaiser "Mr. Kaiser."

Art Linkletter was invited to Mr. Kaiser's home. They began talking and Mr. Kaiser was calling him Art. And Art thought, "He called me Art, I guess I can call him Henry." After awhile, Art woke up. He realized others were calling this man Mr. Kaiser. People who were a lot older than Art were calling him Mr. Kaiser! Even Henry's wife was calling him Mr. Kaiser! Art realized he was the only one in the room calling him Henry. So, he said, "Henry, I don't un-

Animal welfare means taking good care of animals and looking after their needs from their point of view.

derstand something. Here I am much younger than you, you are calling me Art and you let me call you Henry. It just doesn't seem right to me." Kaiser, being the gracious man that he was, said, "Art, you can call me whatever you want. The reason these people call me Mr. Kaiser is sort of a mark of the things I have done. It's kind of like Colonel or Captain. It has nothing to do with anything other than that, but you can call me whatever you want. It's just kind of a little token of respect."

Art Linkletter said, "You know what? I *never* called him Henry again!" I think we would all be better served if we showed that kind of respect for each other. Now that we know what each other has endured and gone through, we should call veterinarians and farriers by their respectful titles.

We should be also courteous to one another. Dr. Robert Miller, a veterinarian from Thousand Oaks, California, says that the most important characteristic of the ideal client is courtesy. They won't call on you at inconvenient times and expect service without

Animal rights means animals are equal to, or more valuable than, humans and deserve the same rights as humans do.

compensation. Also, they won't expect you to put your life in danger.

You can glean great internal satisfaction from helping helpless animals and working with the people who care for them. But the satisfaction quickly evaporates if people don't respect you as a professional. I know a lot of farriers and veterinarians who feel slighted in that way. Farriers are looked down upon because of the dirty and physical nature of their work. See how much respect you get when you go into a closed-in area after you've been working on thrushy horses all day! Similarly, veterinarians are looked down upon by the medical community. They say vets aren't "real doctors." That hurts, especially when, for many years, it was more difficult to get into vet school than med school!

10. Leadership and Handling Options

Most states, by law, give the leadership role for a case to the veterinarian. Perhaps one of the best ways to foster respect is to allow that to occur naturally, even if the owner isn't sure how he or she wants to proceed. This not only shows respect, but also transfers responsibility. That way, if there is trouble down the road, it is not in your lane! ("I just did what you told me, doc!")

When discussing a case, avoid putting the owner in the middle.

Discuss the possible solutions among yourselves and agree on some options. Then let the veterinarian present them to the client with the farrier verifying the prescription.

Recognize there are some people you just can't work with. For various reasons, you just can't communicate with them. It is not your responsibility to work with everybody. But it is your job to be courteous and polite. Gracefully get out of situations that cause you stress. Don't be afraid to refer work that doesn't fit you. Not everyone can do therapeutic work; it takes a lot of skill and experience. Instead, refer work until you can tackle it yourself with confidence and competence. Price your work according to your value. Let the client make the decision. People will afford what they want to afford.

Dr. George Platt, of Edwards, Colorado, told me the following scenario. Dr. Platt has worked on many founder cases as a vet. Here is what he suggests.

> *People will afford what they want to afford.*

> *"I am called to the barn to see a horse that is foundered. He has a serious foot problem. Granted, he has a medical problem, too, and it is my job to take care of that. I ask the owners who their farrier is. I*

don't know this farrier, but I see some other work he has done there, and I don't think he is up to solving this problem. I tell them this is very serious and they need a farrier who specializes in this field. I know one, I will recommend him, and I tell them it will probably cost about $300 to do this job. After they start breathing again, they tell me to call him. The farrier comes out, does the work and presents a bill for $250. The owners are satisfied, the horse recovers and I'm happy.

"Here is another scenario, the more common one of the two. A veterinarian goes into the barn and sees the horse is foundered. He or she clearly can see this horse needs some specialized farrier work. He or she recommends a guy who works a day job, sacks groceries at night, but usually can come on Saturday. He will probably charge only about $30. The guy comes out. He is really not very accomplished at this, it takes a long time, he doesn't get it quite right, and it is more work than he usually does, so he charges $75. The vet has mud on his

face, the farrier has mud on his face, the other farrier, who normally works in the barn, is mad because that is what he usually charges to shoe a horse."

I believe we need to rethink how we handle these problems. Not all farriers can deal successfully with therapeutic cases. It takes a lot of experience and skill. Certain people who are good at it may live several hours away. So, in addition to telling people how much the farriery will cost, explain it will cost that much again to get the farrier to the horse. Then they can make an informed decision.

Let me emphasize again that people will afford what they want to afford. I have been amazed by this. I will say, "It looks like this job is going to cost you several hundred dollars." I think they are going to say no. And they say, "Yes. Is that all?" If they want the value and skill of a top farrier, they will pay for it. Other times, I have cut the price completely to the bone, I'm just doing it because I want to see the horse get well, and I want to help the client. Then they say, "It's too much. Let's bury him." So my advice is to present the options, then let your client decide.

> **Rapport is defined as harmony and understanding that establishes trust.**

11. Understanding Encourages Communication

Farriers and veterinarians are motivated by similar things. They both want to help the animal and provide the best solution for its welfare. They both want to make a living doing what they like to do. They both want respect for doing what they do and for what they have been through to get where they are. They want respect from the client, from the public and from each other. Edgar A. Guest, a poet who wrote *Collected Verse*, published in 1934, said it this way:

Rapport is defined as harmony and understanding that establishes trust.

> When you get
> to know a fellow,
>
> Know his joys
> and know his cares,
>
> When you come to
> understand him
>
> And the burdens
> that he bears,
>
> When you've learned
> the fight he's makin'
>
> And the troubles
> in his way,
>
> Then you'll find
> that he is different
>
> Than you thought
> him yesterday.

We could all do better than we have working together to serve our clients and their horses. One important way to expand our service base is to seek out veterinarians with whom we can effectively work.

Get Training in Communications

Dr. Lydia Miller says that veterinary school graduates "have a strong knowledge base, moderate professional skills and probably no interpersonal communication abilities." The same could be said of many practicing farriers. Communication skills need to be developed.

Dr. Miller, a veterinarian from Illinois, quotes Dr. Cecelia Soares as saying that rapport is most important of the four keys to effective communication, followed by interpretation, empathy and listening. Rapport is defined as harmony and understanding that establishes trust.

She recommends the following sequence be followed to establish rapport when first meeting a client:

1. Introduce yourself.

2. Give your job title.

3. Greet the client *and* animal by name.

4. Offer to shake hands.

5. Maintain a pleasant expression.

6. Make eye contact.

7. Mirror the client's body language and voice tone.

Recognize that it is more important *how* something is said, than *what* is said. Concentrate on the person and give them your full attention for a few minutes. Figure out exactly what they want and try to provide it for them. Adapt your conversation style and professional role to each client. Their lifestyle will affect the effectiveness of the prescribed treatment and client follow-up. Dr. Myrna Milani has written a book called *The Art of Veterinary Practice: A Guide to Client Communication* that discusses the roles and goals of client communication. This book provides much-needed guidance for improving your communication skills.

The Therapeutic Triad

Always think in terms of the other person's victories, needs and fears. Another way of saying this is to be aware of the strengths, limitations and concerns of others. By comparing these lists, you can be better prepared to be empathetic (feel what the other is feeling) and make necessary communication adjustments. Being courteous, humble and teachable.

Stress the synergistic or team approach; it always wins. I call this the therapeutic shoeing triad.

Farrier
Strengths
- Practical experience
- Knows mechanics
- Has no regulation

Limitations
- Mostly right mode thinkers
- Visual learners
- Practical – fast decision makers

Concerns
- Lack formal education
- Limited to mechanical options
- Expectations higher than skill level

Veterinarian
Strengths
- Formal education
- Knows medicine
- Licensed

Limitations
- Mostly left mode thinkers
- Auditory learners
- Scientific – slow decision makers

Concerns
- Lack practical experience
- Limited to medical options
- Education/preparation not valued

Client

Strengths
- Controls capital
- Knows horse
- Makes choices

Limitations
- Most are right mode/ left mode thinking
- Emotional approach to animal
- Looking for immediate and lasting results

Concerns
- Dislikes trainer/veterinarian/farrier conflict
- Horse's welfare not first priority of practitioners
- Lacks scientific and practical knowledge

There may be other factors in the equation when dealing with therapeutic shoeing problems. I suggest you break them down in the same way we have the others so you can better understand them. Then devise a strategy to effectively work with them.

Chapter 13

How to Build Profitability into Your Business

Chapter 13

How to Build Profitability into Your Business

Skilled Farriers Are Well-Paid

Sure, it takes many years to become a skilled farrier. And it is dirty, hard physical work. But the income possibilities for a highly skilled farrier are comparable to a white collar professional.

The following chart from *USA Today*, Feb 22, 2000, gives you some comparisons on earnings. Note: You can determine your own hourly wage by calculating your expenses per horse, then figuring out how long it takes to put each horse through your business (including travel time), then multiplying it by the number of horses.

Get Organized

Those business people who are well-organized have greater potential for earning and keeping their money. A great way to learn organizational skills is by taking a course in time and life management. For example, you can get the basics from one of many books on time management or take one of the courses such as a Franklin Covey course that is regularly offered in major cities. Course in-

What People Make

Occupation	Hourly wage
Fast-food cooks	$6.29
Service station attendants	$7.34
Nursing aides, orderlies	$8.31
Janitors	$8.44
Retail sales people	$9.12
Landscaping, groundskeepers	$9.22
Preschool teachers	$9.39
Secretaries(excludes legal, medical)	$11.86
Roofers	$13.63
Automotive mechanics	$13.97
Heavy-truck drivers	$14.08
Machinists	$14.35
Carpenters	$15.20
Firefighters	$15.63
Mail carriers	$16.39
Tool and die makers	$18.16
Loan officers, counselors	$20.05
Insurance underwriters	$20.42
Computer programmers	$25.67
Physical therapists	$27.49
Chemical engineers	$29.44
Physicists, astronomers	$33.23
Lawyers	$36.49
Dentists	$44.40
Physicians, surgeons	$49.05

Source: Bureau of Labor Statistics
USA Today, Feb 22, 2000, pg 7B

structors talk about time management as the *control of events*. Time management is organizing and executing around priorities. Setting up a filing system that alphabetically stores important correspondence, resource material and tax information is essential. Since time is money, finding material quickly when it is needed is a big time and money saver. I recommend setting up your system to coincide with the categories and levels discussed in Chapter 6.

Articles on various subjects can be filed by category, stored in a notebook(s), and carried in your shoeing rig. These are most useful when the client has a question that requires a long answer, or when you need a written source to back up a statement you've made. Pictures of successful cases you have worked on can also be organized in a notebook to help you sell yourself and your services to the client.

A good deal of thought and planning should go into laying out the back of your truck. A clean and well-organized rig impresses the client, as well as increases your efficiency. Shoe racks, tool hangers and parts organizers can keep materials easy to find and available when you want them. You can spend the time to build your own rig or you can pay someone to make one. Make sure the result is cost-effective and serves your purposes.

This business quiz helps you assess how organized you are.

Business Quiz #1

1. You are often late to shoeing appointments and meetings.
    ☐ True   ☐ False

2. Your shoeing work is constantly being interrupted.
    ☐ True   ☐ False

3. You don't return phone calls from horse owners in a timely fashion.
    ☐ True   ☐ False

4. You can't find what you need in your truck when you need it on the job.
    ☐ True   ☐ False

5. You feel you are losing control of your farrier work
    ☐ True   ☐ False

6. You don't have a life outside of your shoeing work.
    ☐ True   ☐ False

7. You don't know how to say no to prospective shoeing clients.
    ☐ True   ☐ False

8. You don't know how much money you have.
    ☐ True   ☐ False

9. You have a number of over-due farrier supply house bills because you haven't time to get to them.

   ☐ True   ☐ False

10. You have stacks of paper everywhere.

    ☐ True   ☐ False

Any "True" answers indicate you could benefit from organizing skills.

Adapted from Kathleen Allen, *Time and Information Management That Really Works*

Become More Profitable

There are two well-known ways to become more profitable. One is to *reduce expenses* by cutting costs or becoming more efficient. The other is to *increase income* by raising prices or increasing quantity of sales. You can reduce expenses by buying supplies in quantity and scheduling appointments geographically. You can add on mileage to reduce truck expense. You can also increase income by charging more for your services and selling each product you supply separately. The following sections discuss how to price your services.

A good practice is to politely turn down work that is above your skill level or below your going rate.

Set the Right Price for Services

How should a farrier set his/her fees? Setting fees involves several factors. You must consider your skill and experience, your position in the environment in which you practice, your competition and your hunger for work and desire to learn.

One of the most important things a farrier can do is establish a fee structure that will build a sustainable business. Do it wrong, and you get all of your business at the same time – the first time will be the last time! Fees must be fair to both the client and the farrier in the long run. When you're first getting established, your fee should be less than that of an established pro. See yourself in an upwardly spiralling progression for positioning. Ideally, the pros will pass on to the less experienced farrier the potential clients who don't appreciate their services, and the novice will refer the more complex cases to the pro. A good practice is to politely turn down work that is above your skill level or below your going rate.

Why do farriers charge low prices? Here are some common reasons:

1. Low overhead – don't need the money.

2. Don't feel right about charging for service.

3. Uncomfortable asking for money from friends.

4. Feel inferior due to lack of education or credentials.

5. Feel inferior to established names in the business.

6. Afraid of client/business loss if they raise prices.

Business Quiz #2

1. I feel guilty charging friends, neighbors or nice people for what I do.

   ☐ True   ☐ False

2. It has been more than a year since I raised my rates.

   ☐ True   ☐ False

3. I can't afford an annual family vacation or health and life insurance.

   ☐ True   ☐ False

4. I don't buy the magazine subscriptions, equipment or attend the clinics I need to keep me on top of my profession.

   ☐ True   ☐ False

5. I often win new clients on price alone.

   ☐ True   ☐ False

6. I now know a lot more about my business and have a lot more skill than when I began charging the rate I now charge.

   ☐ True   ☐ False

7. My competitors, who are at or below my level of competence and experience, often charge more than I do.

   ☐ True   ☐ False

8. I am always too busy with work that seems to get backlogged.

   ☐ True   ☐ False

9. I find myself doing too much unprofitable "busy" work for my clients.

   ☐ True   ☐ False

10. I'm not sure my work is worth more than I'm charging.

    ☐ True   ☐ False

"Yes" answers to two or more of the above statements indicate a good chance you aren't charging enough for your work.

Adapted from Linda Stern, "Raise Your Rates," *Home Office Computing*, Sept 1996.

What happens when you don't charge enough for your services?

1. You starve your business slowly or you kill it fast.

2. You won't be taken seriously by people with valuable horses.

3. You will waste your time with "nickel-and-dime" clients who sap your creativity and motivation.

4. You won't be able to afford the tools you need to keep your business professional.

5. You will work for too many hours for too little money.

How to Overcome Objections

For each of the objections someone may come up with, you should have a ready answer that shows how they will benefit by being your client. Memorize all the elements so you can repeat it back when the subject comes up.

Begin by agreeing with them. Then tell them how you can be of benefit to them. If they can see that the value of your service is greater than the cost, they will buy it. Try to exceed their expectations.

Here is an example of a benefit statement I have used when someone says, "I will find someone else. You are too expensive."

I can understand that you want to get the best value you can find. I appreciate that because I would do the same thing myself. There are other farriers who charge less. Most will try to do a good job. In fact, I have trained many of the farriers in this area. But when you bring your horse to me, you get more than price. You get me. I come with the deal. You are paying for 40 years of training and experience that has made me one of the most qualified farriers in the world. My specialty is horse shoeing, not just hoof shoeing. I consider the whole horse.

Everything I do is based upon proven principles that will bring you guaranteed results. I am here to serve you and the horse(s) you love by providing excellent, humane care. In the long run, you will save time and money, since problems won't be misdiagnosed and shoes won't be lost due to poor fit. I guarantee my work so if a shoe is accidentally pulled before it is time to reshoe, I will replace it free. I want you to be satisfied with my service, since I intend to be here for a long time and am preparing my son to take over the business.

When you add up my training, experience and achievements and feel the concern I have for you and your horse, you'll discover that I provide the BEST value available.

Estimating the Value of a Horseshoeing Job

A simple way to estimate the value of a basic horseshoeing job done by a beginner is to use the Barber Shop Formula. Multiply the cost of a haircut by eight. For example, if haircuts cost $9, then shoeing should be about $72. Trimming should be about one-third the price of shoeing, or $24. Most farriers can do about three trims in the time it takes to shoe one horse. You could give discounts for a large quantity of work; however, many farriers elect not to do this, as each horse takes the same amount of time and effort.

In the same way, some people choose to go to a higher-priced hair stylist rather than a barber. Position yourself as a "stylist" instead of a "barber."

Tools and Supplies

Tools and supplies increase in cost at least at the rate of inflation. They may go up more due to increases in labor, materials or shipping costs. For example, a pair of high quality hoof nippers used to cost twice as much as a basic shoeing. That is still not a bad gauge to determine the average shoeing cost for a beginner in America. If the suggested retail price for a high quality 15" hoof nipper is $146, the shoeing price should be about $72.

Hourly Billing

Follow these steps to determine an hourly billing.

1. Estimate the annual salary you want to bring home or consider what you made at a salaried job.

2. Add 40% to cover self-employment taxes, health benefits and expenses.

3. Divide by 1,250 — standard number of billable hours a year for self-employed.

4. Example:

   Desired income is $45,000.
   Add 40% to get $63,000.
   Divide by 1,250 hours.
   Hourly rate = $50.40 per hour.

Another way of establishing price for your work is the YECH system, devised by Ken Norkin, as described by Linda Stern's article "Raise Your Rates."

Y - You. How experienced are you? How good are you? What do you offer (that others don't)?

E - Environment. What will the market bear? Where do you live? (What is the climate in the industry)?

C - Competition. What is it? What do they charge? What services do they provide?

H - Hunger. How badly do you need the work or the client? (How much do you want to learn?)

Linda Stern discusses a shortcut method for determining fees that was devised by Ken Norkin. He suggests starting with your salary needs and dividing by the reasonable number of billable hours in a year. Overhead expenses will run between 25% and 33%. This must be added to your target salary. Lowering overhead is one way to increase profit.

If you choose to aim for $50,000 a year, add an average of 28% or $14,000 to it to cover expenses. Thus, your true earnings target would be $64,000. This must be divided by the number of hours you expect to bill a year to get the billing rate. Norkin figures there are 1,000 billable hours in a year.

Here is how he comes up with that number. There are 2,080 hours in a work year (40 hours a week, 52 hours a year). Subtract 100 hours for two and a half weeks of vacation, 80 hours for 10 holidays and 40 hours for sick leave. This leaves 1,860 hours. Marketing (making and confirming appointments on the telephone and visiting clients where no work is done) will take up to 20% to 25% of your time (23% is 419 hours). Administrative tasks, such as accounting, ordering supplies and reading trade publications, will take another 5% (93 hours). Down time, when you are willing to work but it is bad weather or your truck is in the shop, could be as much as 15% (279 hours), and you will probably waste at least 15 minutes a day (58 hours). This gives you about 1,011 billable hours a year in which to earn your salary. Round down to 1,000, and your $64,000 salary comes down to a $64 hourly rate. That compares extremely well with professionals listed on the chart at the beginning of this chapter.

Inflation and Raising Fees

Prices for shoeing should reflect cost-of-living adjustment or inflation increase that occurs each year. These figures are widely published and should be part of your pricing strategy. Chuck Rathmann, in his article "Are your shoeing prices keeping up with inflation?" in Nov. 1998, *American Farriers Journal*, showed that in the last 20 years, shoeing prices should have increased about $80 (from $50 to $130) to keep up with inflation. Inflation continues to be about 3% a year.

The best reason to raise prices is because you have changed. You know more. You have obtained more education. You work faster. You are more skilled. You are more confident. You have achieved mastery at a higher level.

Raising your price should be done one of two ways. You can raise it a small amount each year to reflect inflation or other increased expenses, or you can raise it every few years when you "catch up" and reflect your new level of competence. It is best to raise your prices during the busy season; most clients won't even notice. Always indicate how much the job will cost before you begin, especially with new clients.

Always indicate how much the job will cost before you begin, especially with new clients.

Selling Long-Term Value

Here is a tip that could make you a six-figure shoer immediately. Mostly, it is a joke that demonstrates a person's tendency toward short-sighted thinking. Using this approach in good fun could help you teach the value of looking at the long term.

Next time someone complains about how much it costs to shoe a horse, you might jokingly respond, "I'll make you a deal. Instead of charging my usual price, I will charge by the nail. It will be one cent for the first nail and then double the price for each nail thereafter. One cent for the first, two cents for the second, four cents for the third, eight cents for the fourth, and so on. There are 32 nail holes in the four shoes and I'll use only 24 nails if you like."

Twenty-four nails (six per shoe) will cost $83,886 and 32 nails will cost $21.4 million!

1 = $.01	11 = $10.24	21 = $10,485.76
2 = $.02	12 = $20.48	22 = $20,971.52
3 = $.04	13 = $40.96	23 = $41,943.04
4 = $.08	14 = $81.92	24 = $83,886.08
5 = $.16	15 = $163.84	25 = $167,772.16
6 = $.32	16 = $327.68	26 = $335,544.32
7 = $.64	17 = $655.36	27 = $671,088.64
8 = $1.28	18 = $1,310.72	28 = $1,342,177.28
9 = $2.56	19 = $2,621.44	29 = $2,684,354.56
10 = $5.12	20 = $5,242.88	30 = $5,368,709.12
		31 = $10,737,418.24
		32 = $21,474,836.48

Announcing A Price Increase

You can mail notices to all names in your client base, stating your new prices and policies. You can figure at least 10% will drop out of your circle because of this. But you can also increase your client base by 10% or more by aggressive marketing and creative referrals.

Here is an example of a policy change and expectations list I have used with my clients. I keep the supply price list in my truck billing book for reference, not display.

Butler Farrier Services

Expectations:
What You Can Expect From Us

1. *We will act with integrity, honesty and openness in our relationship with you.*

2. *We will arrive ready to work at the appointed time.*

3. *We will notify you immediately if we are unavoidably detained.*

4. *We will call the day before to remind you of our appointment.*

5. *We will return phone calls in a timely manner and at least within 24 hours.*

6. *We will share current information that will help you better care for your horse.*

7. *We will discuss options and fees for therapeutic work in advance.*

8. *We will refer you to another equine professional, if we believe it will be in your horse's best interest.*

9. *We will treat you and your horse with respect. If working on your horse becomes unsafe for the horse, or us, we will advise you of options before proceeding.*

10. *We will do our best to meet and exceed your expectations, as we believe you are the sole judge of our performance.*

What We Expect From You

1. *You will be open, frank and honest with us.*

2. *You will be committed to providing for your horse's welfare.*

3. *You will provide us with all the information that we need to help your horse.*

4. *You will take time to be present, or arrange for your representative to be present, when we work with your horse(s).*

5. You will provide a safe, dry, level and well-lighted place to work.

6. You will listen to and give our advice due consideration; however, we acknowledge your right to reject our advice.

7. You will pay your account upon receipt unless other mutually agreed-upon arrangements are made in advance.

8. You will refer others to us whom you believe would benefit from our services.

Benefits:

- We run a professional business with a fully stocked mobile shop.

- We service by appointment select clients who desire top quality hoof care.

- Dr. Doug Butler is an expert farrier with 40 years of experience in all fields of farriery and equine science, practicing at the highest level. Jacob Butler is a certified farrier with 5 years of experience.

Conditions:

- Payment is expected at time of service.

- Someone must be available to catch and hold the horse(s) and present payment.

- The location must be a safe, well-lighted, comfortable place to work.

- Horses must be trained and well mannered. Work will be stopped when horses present a safety hazard. Training charges may be added if physical restraint is necessary. We will stop work if the situation becomes unsafe for us or the horse. Veterinary services to administer chemical restraint must be arranged for in advance.

- A 24-hour notice prior to appointment must be given for any appointment changes. This includes: adding or subtracting horse(s) from the appointment scheduled, changing what is scheduled to be done to the horse, canceling an appointment, etc. (after 24 hours, a change fee of $_____ may apply).

- Travel is added according to the following mileage schedule.

Farrier Service Mileage Fee Schedule

We desire to be consistent and fair in mileage charges to our clients. We charge mileage if you are out of the Fort Collins area. This fee is based on one dollar per minute one way. It is determined by the length of time it takes to get to the destination. For example, if it takes 30 minutes to drive to an appointment from Fort Collins, a mileage fee of $30.00 is applied to your farrier fee.

Your mileage fee will be $_____ per visit.

The mileage fee is based on the following factors:

- *Time involved reaching destination (minimizes shoeing time available for the day).*
- *Extra fuel for hauling heavy equipment and tools needed for shoeing.*
- *Truck expense and maintenance.*

Overnight Charges

If two or more days are required to shoe several horses, an overnight charge will be added to your bill. Overnight charges cover expenses to stay the night. The overnight charge is a flat fee of $_____ per night and will be collected at the same time the shoeing bill is paid.

Long Distance Shoeing

Tickets for air travel, mileage to and from Denver International Airport and overnight charges for food and lodging are paid for by the horse owner. A suitable area with forge and anvil must be supplied. We will bring hand tools.

Cost of Supplies Added to Price of Shoeing

Item	Price per Pair
Flat keg shoes fit cold	$
Clipped and forged flat keg shoes	$
Welded clips on shoes	$
Steel training plates	$
Aluminum racing plates	$
Aluminum eventers	$
Aluminum egg bar shoes	$
Titanium egg bar shoes	$
Sliding plates	$
Handmade open shoes	$
Egg bar shoes	$
Heart bar shoes	$
Patten bar shoes	$
Hospital plates	$
Crack patch	$
Glue on shoes	$
Bar wedge pads	$
Snow rim pads	$
Leather full pads	$
Pads in a stack	$
Double nail pads (leather & plastic)	$
Double nail pad application	$
Exposed or under-pad lead	$
Light toe weights	$
Heavy toe weights	$
Bands	$
Silicone packing under pads	$
Quick Poly hoof repair	$
Equipak	$
Studs (4)	$
Tapping (4)	$
Borium	$
Draft keg shoes	$
Draft pads	$
Draft handmade shoes	$

Analyzing Horseshoeing Costs

Another way to figure your rate per horse is to figure your costs on the job. These figures are based on shoeing 1,000 horses a year. Figure how much you spend in each of these categories and divide by 1,000.

This number was calculated by allowing 20 working days every month, with an average of three weekdays per month that are non-productive due to buying supplies, sick days or bad weather. So, 20 days x 12 months = 240 days x 4 to 5 horses per day = 960 to 1,200 horses, or an average of 1,000 horses per year.

Another way to calculate your production days is to subtract from 365 days in a year: 105 weekend days, 8 holidays, 5 sick days, 2 personal days, and 10 vacation days. This is a total of 130, making 235 productive days; 235 days times 4 to 5 horses per day = 940 to 1,175 horses or an average of 1,000 horses per year. If each horse is shod 5 times a year = 200 horses minimum necessary to run a sustainable business.

Of course, trims must be accounted for. Figure that three trims equal one shoeing. So if you had all trims, you should work on 15 horses instead of 5 to get the same income figures.

The following chart illustrates how one arrives at actual take-home pay on a per horse basis. Present example numbers are based on prices in the year 2000.

Item	Present Example	My Business NOW	Future Example	My Business Future
Shoeing Labor Price / horse	75.00		150.00	
Nails (.10 x 40 nails)	4.00		4.00	
Mobile shop purchase, maintenance, insurance	10.00		20.00	
Tool purchase, maintenance	2.00		3.00	
Forge fuel	.25		.50	
Advertising (ads, greeting cards, educational gifts)	3.00		5.00	
Insurance (health, accident, liability)	6.50		9.50	
Vacation/sick leave	9.00		19.00	
Retirement (savings)	7.50		15.00	
Office (secretary, phone, accounting)	9.75		27.00	
Continuing education (schooling, association dues, clinics, subscriptions, career consulting)	2.00		5.00	
Supplies (shoes, pads, studs, etc)	- add on		- add on	
Specific case consulting, evaluation	- add on		- add on	
Excess mileage fee	- add on		- add on	
Per horse business expenses TOTAL	$54.00		$108.00	
Per horse wage and business profit TOTAL	$21.00		$ 42.00	
Taxes (federal and state)	$ 8.40		$ 16.80	
TAKE HOME PAY	$12.60		$ 25.20	

Calculating Costs

Some farriers choose to include the price of the shoes in the cost of the shoeing. They say that way they can make the choice if new shoes are needed. The general rule is if the horseshoe is more than one-half worn through, it should be replaced.

Others add costs for the shoes separately. One reason is that the client then knows the majority of the cost is for your knowledge and skill, not for shoes or supplies. Another reason is that different shoes are required for different types of work. The client can make the choice, not you. This way, your supply cost varies, but your labor stays constant. Generally, this method seems more fair than including the shoes. Extra time for modifying or fitting supplies should be built into the supplies themselves.

The following points explain certain costs more fully. Fill in the blanks and compare your take-home pay with the chart at the beginning of this chapter.

- Nail cost is calculated figuring that nails now cost the farrier about 5 cents each. Carrying the nails in stock makes it necessary to double the cost of the nails to make it profitable to carry them. Shoes should be added on as extra, but the same applies to them. Since more nails will be used than the number of holes in the shoes, I figure two extra nails per foot or 40 total times 10 cents each for $4.00.

- Mobile shop purchase, maintenance and insurance vary with each situation. Farriers who charge lower prices may have lower overhead since they keep their vehicles longer. Maintenance costs may be higher, but insurance costs are lower. The higher figure can be calculated by figuring a new truck kept for three years, with the national average for annual mileage of 25,000 miles. Excess mileage need not be calculated as it is added where extensive travel is required.

- Tool purchase and maintenance includes rasps, knives, nippers, power hand tools and equipment replacement. The total cost is divided by the number of horses shod.

- Forge fuel is based on the cost of propane per gallon. More would be used when shoes are made or require extensive modification.

- Advertising expenses include costs for business cards, reminder cards, postage, flyers, holiday greeting cards, ads in horseshow programs and newspapers, and so on. Gifts for new customers or appreciation for old ones should be included.

- Insurance includes health, disability and liability. Comprehensive liability is advised. Workman's compensation is required in most states. Displaying a copy of your state's equine liability statute is necessary in many states.

- Vacation and sick leave must be figured in to pay for when you can't or don't work.

- Retirement savings should total about 10% of your income and be placed in savings or tax deferred plans.

- Office includes supplies for running the office and hiring office help. This may be part-time services or an accountant, appointment secretary or bookkeeper. A bigger business needs a full-time employee(s).

- Continuing education is essential for farriers. This takes time and means days away from the business. This includes association dues, subscriptions, clinics and seminars. Expert professional business and legal advice is included here.

- Taxes are figured from the wages and profit you make after expenses. If we figure 33% federal income tax and 7% state income tax that is about 40%.

- Take-home pay is how much of the total you actually can spend on personal living expenses for you and your dependents.

Managing Truck Expenses

According to Ford Trucks Fourth Quarter 1999 *Business* magazine, it costs 5 to 10 cents a mile to operate a truck. But the cost of the vehicle, especially the depreciation, must also be figured in. They say the optimum time for trade-in is two-and-a-half to three years or 65,000 to 75,000 miles. The *American Farriers Journal* says the average farrier drives about 480 miles a week or 24,000 miles a year. (At 60 miles per hour, that is eight hours of non-productive time during the business week.)

What are the pros and cons of leasing a truck? Leasing can be profitable if you turn the truck in every two or three years. The higher the mileage, the more attractive leasing is. If you take out the bed liner and store it or put on a custom-made box, you can return the truck in excellent condition. If you intend to keep the vehicle for several years until it is fully expensed off, say in five or 10 years, purchasing makes more sense. The amount of value left after the vehicle is expensed off is the capital recovery charge.

All small items can be expensed at a standard five-year straight-line rate (i.e., divided by five). After five years, they would be worth zero. A dependable vehicle with no debt will increase your bottom line, but it also takes away any deduction for interest and makes your tax bill higher.

Reducing Costs

Be practical as you try to keep job costs down. High quality hand and power tools are usually the best buy. Often, you can save money by buying them used. Used, high quality tools are a better value than new, discounted, poor quality tools.

> *When considering high-ticket items such as trucks and computers, be sure to check with your accountant first.*

Shoes that require less alteration and provide desirable features are often the more economical than inexpensive ones that require a lot of modification. Supplies can often be bought at a discount in quantity.

When considering high-ticket items such as trucks and computers, be sure to check with your accountant first. When you get into the higher tax brackets, it is usually best to upgrade frequently. That way, you can take a larger tax deduction and have the latest "toys." This policy also usually helps to reduce replacement costs at the same time it reduces your tax bite.

Money Matters Summarized

Set a minimum job fee and state it up front for your prospective clients. Give them the choice. If you accept a small job, calculate your time and expense from the time you begin until the time you end. Be careful not to get into situations where you can't afford to meet your expenses. For example, it is not a good idea to work for clients who live long distances away if there are serious high maintenance problems.

Remember, once you establish your rate, that most successful business people regularly turn down 10% of the work that comes their way. This practice gives you time to give exceptional service to those clients who appreciate and value your work. Only change the base rate when the clients provide important concessions that justify it – if they bring the horse to you or allow a helper to work on it, for example.

One of the most successful farriers I know says he sets a goal each year based on his last year's earnings. He decides how much he wants to make and then figures out how much he will have to make per day to reach the target. He then sets up his appointments so he will do the amount of work each day that will bring in the desired amount. He has reached his goals consistently over the years.

Once you establish a fair price, continually resell your clients on your value. Help them remember you by re-membering details about them, their horses and their family. You create value in the customers' minds by being inter-ested in them. Treat your customers as you would treat your mother – since they take care of you.

Remember, even presold customers can be turned off by dress and man-ners. Change shirts frequently on hot days. Clean boots between barns. Wash your hat in the dish-washer. If you are male, shave daily. Use breath mints. Refuse tobacco and alcohol on the job. Remove hat and shoes if you are invited to enter a house. Present a clean bill. Avoid negative talk about others.

Most importantly, make the most of every opportunity to learn and teach. Loan material that you have read. Educate clients on key things you have learned. The only way to do this is to commit to study and apply what you learn every day. If you continually exceed the expectations of your customers, you will be able to serve them for as long as they have horses.

Value vs. Price

Remember that professionals sell value and amateurs sell price.

Treat your customers as you would treat your mother – since they take care of you.

When you obtain a new account, don't celebrate the income you will make; celebrate the cre-ation of a new, mutually beneficial relationship.

Know the job you are to do. If you don't have the confidence to compe-tently complete a job that has been given to you, refer it on to a far-rier who does have the competence and confidence. Expect him or her to refer work to you in return.

Develop an objective for your pricing. Define what you want your business to do for you. Do you want more profit? Do you want to increase sales? Do you want to be a leader in your area? Define what you want and work to get it. Set your price according to your experience and level of competency. Base your price on *their* needs, not just on *your* costs. Help your customers perceive your value. As a farrier, you are a problem solver and a technician. Don't use cost-based pricing. Instead, use perceived-value pricing.

Help clients see how much the problem they have is costing them, how valuable the horse is to them and how much you, a farrier with solutions, can save them. Raise your rates regularly as you develop your ability to be a solution provider.

You must believe you are worth the rates you charge. As one farrier said, "If you put a low value on yourself, rest assured the world will not raise the price." Look in the mirror and ask for a raise. Say, "I'm good. I do good work, I give good service, and I deserve these rates." Put consistent effort into increasing your perceived value.

> *Raise your rates regularly as you develop your ability to be a solution provider.*

Buy Supplies in Quantity

Purchase shoes and other supplies in quantity. Expect a discount for doing so. In addition to these savings, you will save time and fuel by buying in bulk. The most important benefit may be the additional planning required that assures you have supplies on hand in advance of when they are needed. Tools that break or wear out frequently should be bought in pairs.

Build shelves in your shop or garage to arrange your supplies so you can tell at a glance what you have. Storing supplies together in the shop and in the truck makes it easier to find them quickly. Carrying no more than one or two days' supplies in the truck saves fuel and prevents clutter, which is the enemy of efficiency.

Be Part of a Team

Position yourself as an indispensable part of a team that makes horse-owning a pleasure. Other members of the team can be the veterinarian, trainer, barn help, feed merchant, and alternative or complementary therapists. Each must contribute to the satisfaction of owning the horse. Only refer those professionals who you are confident will create this kind of experience for a client.

Multi-Farrier Practices

Multi-farrier practices are becoming more popular. When managed effectively, they can be profitable and allow you to achieve the life balance you desire. They must have systems that create dependable uniformity of service. They should be organized as corporations or other entities for liability protection and tax advantages. The use of Professional Employer Outsourcing (PEO) to handle payroll and benefits is often advantageous. Multi-farrier businesses are usually operated more efficiently and effectively than single-farrier businesses.

Chapter 14

How to Be More Effective in Your Business

Chapter 14

How to Be More Effective in Your Business

Efficiency and Effectiveness

Efficiency and effectiveness are not the same. Efficiency is doing your work with speed and accuracy, defined as skill. Effectiveness is the accomplishment of desired results, defined as business success.

As I have said, the farrier business is not for everyone. I have observed that to be most effective at this ancient and noble craft, the following character traits are essential. I call them the "Seven Habits of Highly Effective Horseshoers." They are adapted from the universal sequential principles of life defined by Dr. Stephen R. Covey in his best-selling book, *The Seven Habits of Highly Effective People*. These habits are not present at birth – they must be developed.

Habits Necessary for Success

1. The Habit of Personal Vision, Attitude Choice or Self-Control

How do you see yourself? Do you consciously create your life? Or do the events of life create you?

Do you control your business? Or does your business control you?

We hear a lot these days about the importance of having vision. What is personal vision? What do people do who have vision?

- They see the total picture or job from beginning to end.

- They visualize what must happen in order to get the results they desire.

- They recognize what they can contribute to the result or solution.

- They consider all the resources and capabilities required to complete the work.

- They conceptualize how these variables need to work together to accomplish the task.

- They are willing to go to work to accomplish their vision.

- They communicate their vision to those around them and motivate others to help them.

- They see what they do as a cause or mission, not a project or task.

Striving to find meaning in one's life is a primary, motivational force for people. A survey of 8,000 students at 48 colleges in the U.S. showed that only 16% thought it was very important to make a lot of money. A majority of 78% said their first goal was finding *purpose* and *meaning* in their lives. This is not something that is invented, but rather something that is detected.

Does your work have meaning and purpose? Is it hard work or is it fun? Nothing is ever work unless you would rather be doing something else. Are you addicted to horseshoeing, a "horseshoeing junkie," as farrier instructor Scott Simpson calls it?

I remember when I was enrolled in the Cal Poly Horseshoeing School, I could hardly wait for each new day so I could learn more and practice the new things I was learning. I loved everything about it – the smell of the horses, the ring of the anvil, the rhythm of the hammer, the heat of the fire, the feel of the tools and the form of the shoes. I also liked talking with clients.

At the time, I was employed as a cowboy, working with livestock and competing in the rodeo rough stock and timed events. I loved that, too, but I knew horseshoeing was going to be my life's work.

Do you like working hard with your hands as much as your head? Do you want to help people enjoy their horses? Do you want to share information and skill to provide a needed service? What is your primary aim?

Michael E. Gerber, author of *The E Myth*, says it this way, "Your primary aim is the vision necessary to bring your business to life and your life to your business. It provides you with a purpose. It provides you with energy. It provides you with the grist for your day to day mill."

Successful business owners choose the attitude they will possess as they build their businesses.

Dr. Viktor Frankl, a psychiatrist and an Austrian Jew imprisoned and tortured by the Nazis during World War II, has said that the greatest of the human endowments is our ability to choose one's attitude in a given set of circumstances. He called this the "ultimate freedom" in his book, *Man's Search for Meaning*. Events

Successful business owners choose the attitude they will possess as they build their businesses.

around you may get out of control (you may lose your liberty), but how you look at the events can remain under your control (you can retain your freedom).

Tolerance for pain is a necessary prerequisite for participation in the farrier business. Pain becomes insignificant (at least less significant) if our work has purpose and meaning.

Henry David Thoreau said, "I know of no more encouraging fact than the unquestionable ability of man to elevate his life by conscious endeavor." Gerber adds to that by saying, "The difference between great people and everyone else is that great people create their lives actively, while everyone else is created by their lives, passively waiting to see where life takes them next."

2. The Habit of Beginning with the End in Mind or Visual Thinking

This is the habit of visualizing and planning the desired result. It is especially important in the farrier business, and for that matter, in any craft. Michelangelo once was asked how he had created the *Pieta*, a beautiful white marble sculpture. He said that he saw (visualized) the figures inside the block of marble, then went about the task of removing all the excess rock around them.

Farriers are often given the task of "sculpturing" a functional thing of beauty from a mass of deformity. We must be able to visualize the desired result. The vision we see guides our hands. The ability to think visually can be developed to some extent, but an artistic sense of form and symmetry, and the ability to visualize, are mostly innate and part of right-brain function. Development of this skill is similar to developing muscles. Everyone has muscles, but only those who train and develop those muscles have the muscular strength and physique that accompanies such effort and sacrifice.

I'm often asked by veterinarians if they should expect farriers to be trained to read radiographs. I say, "Of course not, but always show any radiographs you have to the farrier." Effective farriers are visual people. Good drawings are much better than words as a way of communicating useful information.

I believe in teaching veterinary students, as well as farriers, how to draw and picture things. I learned this valuable skill from Alan Bailey, AFCL, at the National Farrier Training Center in Hereford, England. Pencil control is as difficult to achieve as hammer control. Visual presentation is the basis of the farrier exams in England. I believe verbal testing is a poor way to test visual people like farriers about an artistic subject like horseshoeing.

Several years ago, I became well acquainted with an autistic scientist. *The New Yorker* and *People* magazines wrote articles about her, stating that she is the highest functioning autistic person known to the world of medicine. I speak of Dr. Temple Grandin, an animal science professor at Colorado State University. She is a total visual thinker.

Dr. Grandin has interviewed thousands of people and asked them to describe what they see when she says to "access your memory on church steeples." The variation in responses is amazing. Some see a specific church; others see a drawing or even the letters of the word. She believes a person can only move a short distance on the scale. Apparently, this ability is "hardwired" and can be cultivated to a limited extent, but it must be inherently present for a person to exhibit an artistic sense of form and symmetry in their work. She believes that animals are total visual thinkers, as are autistic savants, and the difference between animals and men is the long-term vision or imagination exhibited by people.

Standards of work are visualized in our minds. They help create the energy by which we produce our best work. Ideally, our work will be so in harmony with our plans (visualized result), that our work is a reflection of us. It is a mirror of our inner vision. I believe this habit strongly influences hand-eye coordination and that lack of awareness and attention to the cultivation of this habit can limit the level of skill we achieve.

3. The Habit of Organizing Around Priorities and Being Consistent in Your Work

Through constant attention and focus, we can develop manual dexterity and rhythm to do our work efficiently. Strength is not enough.

Risk of error and injury to horse or horseshoer is greatly decreased by having a well-thought-out and orderly, rehearsed and practiced protocol for doing every operation. Prior to winning the National Horseshoeing Championship in 1980, I went through a very extensive self-analysis and built many new tools. Then I rehearsed the use of each as part of the overall job. I developed great confidence that served me well. That would be true even if I hadn't won.

For much of my life, I looked at my work for negative things (what not to do) instead of positive things (what to do). This probably comes from my university training.

I had a major paradigm shift one day when I was talking to

Pennsylvania farrier, Dave Duckett. I asked him the obvious question. Why are you so good? (There was a time when he was nearly unbeatable in competition. I first met him in 1980, and had the privilege of being his competition partner in 1986 when we won the English national title.) He taught me this great principle: "I do what I do the same way, every time. The same steps, the same track of the mind." I later learned when I traveled to England with him that this "track" was developed by many years of practice. I saw the pile of shoes he made as an apprentice and journeyman. It was about eight feet in diameter and 20 feet in height. Duckett said, "When I need to speed up, I just turn up the rheostat on my motor and go faster. Everything is the same; I'm on the same track, I just go faster. If I make a mistake, I have already decided a course of action to correct it. I have organized and prepared my response before I confront the situation. This has allowed me to practice in my mind and come out on top in some tight situations."

I got to see this discipline in action. A few months after this original conversation with Duckett, I was his fireman and

In our type of service, which is creative and repetitive, it's critical to plan our work and work our plan to be effective.

striker at the Closeburn, Scotland, Clydesdale Shoeing Competition. Because I was not used to the coke fire, I burned up two rocker bar specimen shoes. In addition, after making the Clydesdale shoe and fitting it, Dave discovered it was too long. At 35 minutes to go, he said, "Go cut another piece of stock!" We not only finished, but Duckett did a fine job in half the time allotted. Yes, we certainly did have our motors running at high speed!

In our type of service, which is creative and repetitive, it's critical to plan our work and work our plan to be effective. We must orchestrate our ideas into reality. Orchestras practice a good deal before they can play symphonies to perfection. Consistency of product (and satisfaction) are highly desirable. Because horseshoeing is piecework, it must be learned one piece at a time and put together, even as an orchestra is a blending and unification of many artists each playing different instruments.

Ralph Waldo Emerson said, "A man's success is made up of progressive failures which he rises above, because he experiments and ventures every day. And the more falls he gets, the faster he moves on." To use a rodeo analogy, "gapping open" and exposing yourself is the best way to win when riding bareback bucking horses; but it is also the best way to get bucked off!

4. The Habit of Thinking Win-Win or Seeking the Solution that Is in Everyone's Best Interest

This habit applies to dealing with horses, as well as with human clients. William Hunting in his book *The Art of Horseshoeing*, published in the early 20th century, said, "The farrier has not been fairly treated by the public. His practical knowledge has been ignored, he has been instructed by amateurs in all sorts of theories, and coerced into carrying out practices, for the untoward results of which he has been blamed. The natural consequence of all this has been that the art of farriery degenerated, and the farrier was forced into a position destructive to the self-respect of any craftsman. In no other trade do persons, entirely ignorant of the business, presume to direct and dictate as to how the work should be done. No one presumes to instruct the watchmaker or bell-hanger as to the details of his craft, but the farrier has been compelled to take his instructions from all sorts and conditions of men. Only in recent years has the man who shoes horses been allowed to know something of his calling – since when horseshoeing has improved."

When I was teaching horseshoeing at Cal Poly, Pomona, in the late 1960's, I also had the responsibility of shoeing the Arabian show horses there. "Sandez" was a great reining and stock horse that was very toed-in. The management wanted his leg to look straight, and so I twisted his leg using a severe corrective shoe. Over the course of a couple of years, he developed sidebone and ringbone, and became very lame. I got the blame. After that, whenever the management would take a visitor by the turnout pasture, the visitor would ask, "What is that lame horse out in the pasture?" The management's response was consistently, "Oh, that's a horse that the farrier crippled!" I learned from that experience not to go against my better judgment when carrying out client instructions.

We must seek the solution that works best for everyone. We can't always think only of the horse, but must also consider the owner who pays the bill. When dealing with difficult problems, we must ask ourselves if the solution will be of long-term benefit to the horse, to the owner and to the farrier. Most of our good business is repeat business. A solution that makes everyone happy will keep us all coming back together.

A great example of recognizing reality often occurs when training horses. It might appear to be best for the horse if it could run free without restraint or dominance. But, in the horses' community, dominance exists. They are comfortable with being dominated; it is part of the reality of life. Horses that are not taught that man is dominant are not a pleasure for farriers to work with and, therefore, they don't get expert foot care. You might think of survival of the fittest. The "wild" horses get referred to the newest farriers in town!

Learning to read horses and to sense their "comfort" is a very difficult part of our business. It is the most difficult thing to teach. I think it must be developed as a youth by handling and riding many horses. Reading and reacting to a horse includes sensing its motivation and temperament. Several former students have told me that their farrier work improved when they learned to ride horses. One such person was Bryce Laraway from Lake Helen, Florida who bought a horse when he was close to 50 and called it "Second Childhood." He said that learning to ride this horse dramatically improved his farrier work.

5. The Habit of Empathetic Communication or Developing Open Liaison with Veterinarians, Trainers and Owners

This habit involves the principle of diagnosing before prescribing. We must seek to understand the problem, and the other person's point of view before we seek to be understood.

Once I was asked to shoe a horse that was described as one that "don't look too good" because he stumbled. Rocker toes were prescribed and applied. But the horse ran into the wall as he was led out of the shop. That's when I realized it was blind!

Learn to observe, learn to listen. We may think we know the answer, but we must refrain from pushing it on others until they arrive at it themselves. People see the world differently. In addition to the differences between visual and abstract thinkers, people have differences in background and perspective.

Once while I was still a student, I was called to shoe a horse for some people who had just bought their first horse. Without thinking, I recited all my newly learned knowledge by telling them about the lumps and bumps on their horse's legs. They became quite concerned and later called the horse dealer and demanded their money back. He was very upset, as he knew he could never find another horse that fit this family as well as this gentle old horse. I should have kept my mouth shut!

Joe Kriz of Connecticut tells the story of his experience with a new horse owner and a veterinarian. They were examining a horse with a sore foot. The vet said to Joe, "I radiographed this horse, and it has a fractured third phalanx." Joe said, "Okay, Doc. Now you need to tell the owners about it, but they are very new to horses. This is their first horse. You need to tell them in common words that everyone understands." So the vet said, "Sir, Mr. Kriz and I have examined your horse, I've x-rayed the horse, and I'm sorry to report that he has a cracked coffin bone." The owner became very upset and said, "I knew it! I knew this horse was sick! He's been a coffin' every since we bought him!"

We miss the mark a lot by not considering another's point of view because we are too wrapped up in our own thing. Often, other people's different experiences and perspectives will help us achieve a more effective and creative solution than we could have achieved alone. To listen well, we must be sure of ourselves, and see

I had to be willing to change my behavior. Can you change your behavior when it works against you?

our purposes clearly. It also helps to be open and willing to change.

While I was enrolled as a graduate student at Penn State, I worked for the biggest boarding stable in town. I was shoeing all the horses and, by working there once a week, I could make enough to pay for my educational and living expenses. One day, I began to work on a new horse that wasn't as quiet as most. The stable owner, Phil Jodon, walked by and said, "I'm going to lunch. I'll be back shortly." Pretty soon, the horse I was working on acted up for the 14th time and I lost my temper. I kicked him in the belly and recited his pedigree and a few other choice superlatives to get his attention. Then, I picked up my tools and returned to work. Just then, an irate and red-faced Mr. Jodon appeared at the door. He said, "Get your stuff, get out of here, and don't ever come back!" I said, "Okay, as you wish, but would you mind telling me why?" He said, "You see that little box up in the rafters above where you are working? That's what we use to monitor the horses when we're not in the barn. We forgot it was on, and while my family and I were in the very act of saying grace, the most terrible language came into our kitchen, embarrassing me and my family. Now, you either go in and apologize to my family, or don't ever come back!" I apologized and have been more in control ever since. I had to be willing to change my behavior. Can you change your behavior when it works against you?

We must understand that we are building a business, not just improving our skill and product. As Gerber stated in *The E Myth*, "The commodity is the thing your customer actually walks out with in his hand. The product is what your customer feels as he walks out of your business. Understanding the difference between the two is what a successful business is all about... The truth is, nobody is interested in the commodity. People buy feelings... how your business anticipates those feelings and satisfies them is your product."

The head of a large cosmetic company once said, "At our factory we make cosmetics (commodity), in our stores we sell hope (product or benefit)."

We must learn how to read the situation and even turn it into a joke. We could call it "reading the flinches." When a client asks how much you charge to shoe a horse, look the client right in the eye and say, "That will be fifty dollars." If they don't flinch, you say, "That's for the examination." If they say, "Well, how much to shoe the horse?" You look them right in the eye and say, "Fifty dollars." And, if they don't flinch, you say, "That's for trimming the feet and applying the shoes." And then, if they say, "Well, how much for the shoes?" You look them straight in the eye and say, "Fifty dollars." And, if they don't flinch, you say, "Each."

Charlie Halleran, instructor at California City of Industry Horseshoeing School, used to say he counted the Cadillacs in the garage before writing out the bill!

6. The Habit of Creative Cooperation or Synergy – the "Holistic" Habit

The habit of synergy is the fruit of practicing the other habits. It is the point where we blend all of our energy together in a creative way to get an additive effect. Great farriers are always operating in this mode. They bring all of their training and experience to the job at hand, using the skills of others who may be able to help. Colorado farrier, Terry Strevor, says, "They use all of their senses to shoe the horse. I think all good farriers who have learned the craft well become one with the horse. They get inside its skin. They sense its rhythm of life. They are in harmony or balance with it."

When teaching students how to train young horses, I have emphasized the importance of feeling the position of the horse's feet when riding. We work on subconsciously being aware of where the horse's feet are. When I ride a horse to work cattle, I become a part of that horse. We're working in unity, true unity, as Tom Dorrance calls it.

A great orchestra makes different and more powerful music than an individual artist with an individual instrument. Altogether, they make more beautiful and moving music than each could by itself. A harmonic orchestra is a classic example of synergy.

Synergy is everywhere in Nature where the whole is greater than the sum of its parts. Indeed, our relationships with horses are synergistic since we provide for and protect them in return for the joy they give us. We value the differences, and we are both better off by coming together.

7. The Habit of Balanced Self-Renewal

We recognize the four dimensions to our nature: physical, mental, social/emotional and spiritual. They are sometimes called by different names. Philosophers may call them values including tone (physical), autonomy (mental), connectedness (social/emotional) and perspective (spiritual). Running guru George Sheehan calls the physical being a good animal, the mental being a good crafts-

man, the social being a good friend and the spiritual being a saint. Saint Francis of Assisi said, "He who works with his hands is a laborer; he who works with his hands and his head is a craftsman; (but) he who works with his hands, and his head, and his heart is an artist."

Investing in ourselves by renewal includes doing those things that create a balanced life style. For me, it is exercise (muscles other than the back, riding and Western arts), reading at least a book each week, regular family activities and meditation over core values daily.

Learn to prepare so you can have private victories before public performances. The will to prepare is more important than the will to win. Continually educate yourself. By doing these things consistently, you build character. Character formation is a steady, long-continuing process.

Again quoting *The E Myth*, "People who succeed in business don't do so because of what they know, but because of their insatiable need to know more."
Success is not determined by the hand you are dealt – but rather by how you play the hand you are dealt. Our greatest need is yearning power, not earning power.

One person who had yearning power to a high degree was Elihu Burritt, born in New Britain, Connecticut, in 1810. He became widely known as the Learned Blacksmith. All of his spare time was spent in study. He learned Greek and Hebrew so he could study the Bible in the original. By the time he was 21, he could also speak French, German, Italian and Spanish. He moved to Worcester, Massachusetts, after the financial panic of 1837. He went about giving lectures when he wasn't too busy shoeing horses. He eventually taught himself to speak 50 languages. He preached the value of honor, emancipation and world concord. He died in 1879.

My father and I (of course, since I was named after my father) were named after a German immigrant schoolteacher, Karl G. Maeser. He was greatly admired by my grandmother. He was once asked by his pupils what it meant to him to give your word of honor. He explained, "Place me behind prison walls – walls of stone ever so high, ever so thick, reaching ever so far into the ground. There is a possibility that in some way or another, I may be able to escape. But, stand me here on the floor and draw a chalk line around me and have me give you my word of honor never to cross it. Can I get out of that circle? No, never! I would die first!"

I believe that each of us can grow by changing our attitudes and habits.

Success Is Not Easy to Obtain

Obviously, building character true to our vision, living a life of service in our business, and balancing our lives isn't easy. But it is possible. Ralph Waldo Emerson said, "That which we persist in doing becomes easier – not that the nature of the task has changed, but our ability to do has increased." Persistence is a magnificent virtue.

Covey concludes *The Seven Habits of Highly Effective People* by reminding us, "By centering our lives on correct principles and creating a balanced focus between doing and increasing our ability to do, we become empowered in the task of creating effective, useful and peaceful lives... for ourselves, and for our posterity."

Early on in life, I made up my mind to learn all there was to know about each of the phases of horseshoeing. I grabbed opportunities as they came to me, and I've had some great experiences. I believe most of these opportunities came to me because I have an insatiable need to know more. In fact, I learned most of what I know from observing highly effective farriers.

Also, I made up my mind many years ago that I was going to convey that information to people who wanted to be working farriers. I have tried to develop habits of effectiveness. I believe that each of us can grow by changing our attitudes and habits. We can become highly effective if we choose to and work at it.

Farriers are in a unique position. We have one foot in the ancient, self-reliant world of yesterday, but we must make good use of modern materials and technology to be successful today. Our career requires long preparation and hard physical work. Major changes in ourselves are required as we seek to grow and progress and become more effective in our work.

Our lives are much like a bar of iron. The value changes depending on what is made from it. You can make horseshoes, sewing needles or parts for the fine watches from it. The value is increased as labor and machinery is increased. Life is also like a fine watch. It takes a long time to put it together and to tune it. And, finally, life is like a piece of metal against a grindstone. It will either grind you down or polish you up. It all depends on what you are made of.

Chapter 15

How to Balance
Your Business and Your Life

 *Chapter 15*

How to Balance Your Business and Your Life

Seeking Balance

Balance is the most important thing in horseshoeing and in life. We each want it all, but seem unwilling to learn how to make it work. As the popular song says, "Everybody wants to go to heaven, but nobody wants to die."

Studies have shown that most people are motivated by only a few deep cravings or needs (the order varies with individuals):

1. Health
2. Preservation of life
3. Food
4. Sleep
5. Money
6. Life after death
7. Spiritual fulfillment
8. Sexual gratification
9. The well being of our children
10. A feeling of importance

The last one, a feeling of importance, is one that is missing for many people – and it's the one craved the most, according to William James, one of America's most famous psychologists. Keep that in mind every day as you work with people. They will love you for it.

Effectiveness Requires Balance

True effectiveness requires balance. As Stephen Covey said, "Success in one area of life doesn't compensate for failure in another. It can appear to for a limited time. But, success in your profession cannot compensate for a broken marriage, ruined health or character weakness."

Each of us has the responsibility for our own lives. Accepting and living with this responsibility is a major part of becoming effective. Covey also said, "The best way to predict your future is to create it."

"Circumstances may color our lives, but we can choose the color," said Napoleon.

"Be the change you want to see in the world," said Gandhi.

The 10 most powerful two-letter words are, "If it is to be – it is up to me."

We all seem to spend a good amount of our lives worrying about making a living and how we will go about it. Maybe we should take more stock in the advice from Marsha Sinetar's best-selling book *Do What You Love, the Money Will Follow*. She preaches that our lives are created by us; we are in control. She says, "We can't all be stars, but we can all sparkle."

A Stanford University study, quoted in "Win with Your Strengths" by D.O. Clifton and P. Nelson, 1992, *Readers Digest*, found that exceptional intelligence doesn't guarantee extraordinary accomplishment. Instead, it seems clear that spectacular achievers were focused on what they want to do in life.

"Prepare and your chance will come," said Abraham Lincoln. Talent alone doesn't guarantee success. Rather, excellence comes from commitment, hard work over the long term and liking what you are doing. Skill development takes time and results from developing our strengths. In addition, everyone needs support to help make up for weaknesses and give meaning to our lives.

> *Exceptional intelligence doesn't guarantee extraordinary accomplishment. Instead, it seems clear that spectacular achievers were focused on what they want to do in life.*

Time More Valuable than Money

Hilton Hotels did a telephone survey of 1,010 people to determine people's attitudes toward time and money that was reported in *Home Office Computing*, Feb. 1993. The researchers found that most people would give up the security of a steady paycheck in exchange for more control over their life and work.

1. 70% of those earning $30,000 or more a year would give up a day's pay each week for an extra day of free time

2. 38% had cut back on their sleep to make more time

3. 31% worried that they don't spend enough time with family and friends

4. 20% had called in sick at least once last year simply because they needed to relax

What would this group of people like to do if they had more time?

1. 77% would like to spend more time with family and friends

2. 74% would like to improve themselves intellectually, emotionally or physically

3. 72% would like to save more money

4. 68% would like to have free time to spend anyway they please

5. 61% would like to make more money

6. 19% would like to pursue hobbies, travel and do other activities

Effective people learn to use their time wisely. *The Chicago Tribune* published a survey by the A.C. Nielsen Co. cited in the March 17, 1991, issue of the Fort Collins, Colorado, *Coloradoan*. It shows that as income goes up, the number of hours of television viewing goes down. We need to spend more time on our business and personal relationships to be prosperous.

People spell love T-I-M-E.

Goals Help Achieve Success

Income and standard of living are directly related to how we set goals. Writing down specific goals help us:

- Clarify our mission or purpose in life.

- Concentrate on achieving our dreams.

- Accomplish our purposes.

- Increase our self-respect.

- Anticipate success with enthusiasm.

- Make good decisions about the use of time.

- Stay focused on our desired course of action.

Goals clarify our priorities. Often, we say that something is a priority in our life but then our actions don't show it. The source of personal integrity is to align our habits to match our values, make our actions equal to our words.

Spouses/Dependents Want To:	Spouses/Dependents Don't Want To:
a. Be loved	a. Feel neglected/ignored
b. Be healthy	b. Get hurt/have health problems
c. Feel secure	c. Feel insecure/unprotected
d. Have fun	d. Have no time for fun
e. Feel comfortable	e. Feel stressed/out of balance

What we do when no one is watching reveals a lot about us. Integrity is the price we put on being true to ourselves. Shakespeare put it this way: "This above all, to thine own self be true and it follows, as the night the day, thou cans't not then be false to any man."

Extent of Personal Influence

Networking was discussed in Chapter 10 where it was stated that the average person knows 250 people at any one time. It has also been determined that during an average lifetime, a person will directly or indirectly influence the lives of 3,000 people. No one can ever predict the influence one will have on another. Here's a related story.

In the late nineteenth century, a wealthy English family was spending the weekend with a wealthy Scottish family. One of their sons fell into a swimming pool. The boy was about to drown when the gardener plunged in and saved him. The parents were deeply grateful and attempted to reward the gardener. At first he hesitated, but they insisted. The gardener admitted, "I have a son whose dream it is to be a doctor, and we cannot afford to send him to the University." True to his word, the wealthy member of Parliament made it possible for the Scottish gardener's boy to go to medical school.

A little more than a half-century later, a famous world statesman lay near death with pneumonia that he had contracted at a wartime conference in Morocco. The statesman was given the new wonder drug called *penicillin*. It saved his life. Winston Churchill, the late Prime Minister of Britain and the boy who almost drowned, later commented, "Rarely has one man owed his life twice to the same person." Dr. Alexander Fleming, the discoverer of penicillin and winner of the Nobel Prize for Medicine in 1945, was the son of the Scottish gardener (from *Bits and Pieces*, Aug. 1979).

We don't always know of the influence we will have. Author Louisa May Alcott said, "You can count the seeds in an apple, but you can't count the apples in a seed." She used this statement to illustrate the fact that we all affect eternity, since we can never tell where our influence stops. We must give of ourselves in order for our influence to last. Here is a parable written by Olive Schreiner, author of *The Story of an African Farm* (published in the 1920s), for you to ponder.

The Artist's Secret

There was an artist once, and he painted a picture. Other artists had colors richer and rarer, and painted more notable pictures. He painted his with one color; there was a wonderful red glow on it; and the people went up and down, saying, "We like the picture; we like the glow."

The other artists came and said, "Where does he get his color from?" They asked him; and he smiled and said, "I cannot tell you," and worked on with his head bent low.

And one went to the Far East and bought costly pigments, and made a rare color and painted it, but after a time the picture faded. Another read in the old books, and made a color rich and rare, but when he had put it on the picture it was dead.

But the artist painted on. Always the work got redder and redder, and the artist grew whiter and whiter. At last one day they found him dead before his picture, and they took him up to bury him. The other men looked about in all the pots and crucibles, but they found nothing they had not.

And when they undressed him to put his grave-clothes on him, they found above his left breast the mark of a wound—it was an old, old wound, that must have been there all his life, for the edges were old and hardened; but Death, who seals all things, had drawn the edges together, and closed it up.

And they buried him. And still the people went about saying, "Where did he find his color from?

And it came to pass that after a while the artist was forgotten – but the work lived.

Formula for Success

In the early 1960s, the vice-presidents and personnel directors of 100 of the nation's largest corporations were asked what determines if someone will be successful. Their answers listed below showed that hard work was more important than luck (or anything else). Work is something we are all capable of.

- Work – 52%
- Intelligence – 21%
- Undetermined – 10%
- Experience – 9%
- Personality – 6%
- Luck – 0%

Even happiness, that elusive quality that most of us seek, depends upon work. Happiness comes when you can see what you are, and you like what you see.

Mary Lou Retton, winner of the 1984 Gold Medal in Women's All-Around Gymnastics competition, has been quoted as saying, "The little things can make us so stressed. Those are not the things that make you truly happy. It's the relationships we have. It's the attitude we have. Happiness does not come easily. It is effort and work. But, I really believe that all of us can possess it, if we want it … True happiness is where I am right now: having a family who loves me … Happiness is the place I'm in now in my life, not a 16-year-old kid with a gold medal, but a 32-year-old wife and mother who is very secure in who she is and where she is in life."

Overcoming Fears

A lot of what keeps us from happiness is the fear we have of failure. This great poem I memorized in the 1960s when I was at Penn State University describes this problem:

If you think you are beaten,
 you are.

If you think you dare not,
 you don't.

If you'd like to win but think
 you can't,

It's almost certain that you
 won't.

Life's battles don't always go

To the stronger woman or man,

But sooner or later,
 those who win

Are those who think they can.

What are you most afraid of? A team of market researchers asked 3,000 U.S. inhabitants this question. The results, reported in the 1980s, may surprise you.

1.	Speaking before a group	41%
2.	Heights	32%
3.	Insects and bugs	22%
4.	Financial problems	22%
5.	Deep water	22%
6.	Sickness	19%
7.	Death	19%
8.	Flying	18%
9.	Loneliness	14%
10.	Dogs	11%
11.	Driving/riding in a car	9%
12.	Darkness	8%
13.	Elevators	8%
14.	Escalators	5%

According to the *London Sunday Times*, which reported this American survey, "In general, women were far more fearful than men. Twice as many were afraid of heights, insects, deep water, flying or driving in cars; three times as many were frightened of darkness and four times as many were frightened of elevators. They were also more fearful of dogs, of getting sick and of dying. But if that makes it seem like a male chauvinist survey, it is worth noting the only fear that men have more often than women is the fear of financial problems."

I can identify with the number one fear; it was mine for many years. I was very shy as a child and could never talk in front of a group. It was expected in the family and church environment I grew up in, but I could never do it. I would always become very emotional, tearful and physically unable to speak. The speech class required in college was the last one I took before graduation. I had a great coach and he helped me see the value of preparation and practice to overcome my fear. Since then, I have spoken all across the country and in many foreign countries, many times without notes and for several hours or even days at a time.

Overcoming fears, takes dedication, time and work. It is worth the effort, however, as success in business or life is difficult to achieve when fears hold us back.

A Pleasing Personality

Ben Franklin (1706-1790) is a model of someone who realized what he needed to do to become an effective person. Once described as rude and selfish, he realized he must change himself. At 27 years of age, he made a list of 13 virtues taken from his study of the Bible and developed a system for incorporating them into his life. The virtues were temperance, silence, order, resolution, frugality, industry, sincerity, justice, moderation, cleanliness, tranquility, chastity and humility.

He focused on one each week. Many of his sayings, first published in *Poor Richard's Almanac*, are still repeated today. For example, "Early to bed, early to rise, makes a man healthy, wealthy and wise." And, "God helps them who help themselves." And another, "He who falls in love with himself will have no rivals."

It has been said of Ben Franklin, "No other American . . . has done so many things so well." He was a jack of all trades and master of many, including printer, publisher and inventor. He led a long and useful life. He is the only man who signed all four key documents in American history: the Declaration of Independence, the Treaty of Alliance with France, the Treaty of Peace with Great Britain, and the Constitution. He and his wife Debby Read had a synergistic relationship. He helped her; she helped him. They were a devoted couple with three children.

Franklin believed in industry, frugality and thrift. He refused to take out patents on his inventions as he wanted to contribute to the comfort and convenience of people. Some of his inventions were the Franklin Stove, lightening rods,

> *Overcoming fears, takes dedication, time and work.*

bifocals, hospitals, libraries, postal service, daylight saving time, electricity and lime added to acid soil. A neighbor once said of him, "The *industry* of Franklin is superior to anything I ever saw... I see him at work when I go home; he is at work again before his neighbors are out of bed." Franklin said, "Wealth is not his who has it, but his who enjoys it."

A Balanced Life

Jim Rhode, an Arizona businessman, sums up a balanced life as staying healthy, happy and hooked. Divorce is one of the greatest destroyers of financial security and happiness. We must learn how to make money in our business and have fun doing it. And we need to learn all we can, but we must never lose sight of why we're working so hard.

Dave Wixom, as quoted by Dr. Reed Bradford in *A Teacher's Quest* (1971), said, "Education is a personal thing. It is a private love affair. Education is the impact of knowledge as thrust at you by the magnetism of personalities who are the living embodiment of their knowledge, on your personality as you think, not memorize... Education is selective retention. It is the careful assimilation of knowledge in some orderly fash-

Franklin said, "Wealth is not his who has it, but his who enjoys it."

ion toward a meaningful goal, in some conceptual framework, such that each fact is assigned a value in relation to all other facts. Education is the transformation of facts into values. You only have education when knowledge is integrated into the personality and is transformed by that personality into wisdom."

Some things in life are much more important than others. Karl Gauss, the great German mathematician (inventor of the algebraic solution), said, "There are problems to whose solutions I would attach infinitely greater importance than to those of mathematics; for example touching ethics, or our relation to God, or concerning our destiny and future." And there are some things infinitely more important than horseshoeing.

Ted Morris, FWCF, was probably the greatest competitive farrier who ever lived. As members of the North American Horseshoeing Team, we visited him at his home in England in 1986. He showed us his hundreds of gold medals he had won in competition. While others looked at the gold medals, his wife showed me the most precious one he ever won. It was silver and hung around her neck. I asked why it was the most precious one. She said with lots of emotion, "Because it's silver. Silver is second place. He had to come down from first place to win it because I asked him to get me a silver one."

Balance is the most important thing in horseshoeing and in life. A variety of solutions to individual problems is characteristic of good horseshoeing and good music and good life. Good music comes from a harmonic blending of high notes and low notes to suit the individual occasion. Playing of one key makes dull and even distressing music. There are 88 keys on the piano but a thousand symphonies. We all have different tastes in music. But competency in the use of the instrument is necessary to produce any music. It requires years of dedication and effort – not just a few lessons and a little unsupervised practice. Progression is by levels and can be demonstrated by pieces performed at a recital. We put on a recital every day of our lives by the work we do and the way we live.

Trust Is What It's All About

Trust is what we must inspire in clients to build a successful, sustainable business. Trust is what we must inspire in our children and partners in life. What

Balance is the most important thing in horseshoeing and in life.

causes people to trust us? Dr. Carl A. Osborne, a veterinarian, noted 10 reasons why people trust us in the November 15, 1993, issue of the *Journal of the American Veterinary Medical Association.* He draws heavily from his experience in practice and from Covey's works.

He believes that trustworthiness is based on the following 10 principles:

1. Truthfulness – trust is based on truth – we possess the truth and the truth must possess us.

2. Honesty – our words and deeds match our thoughts and actions.

3. Reliability – be punctual and responsible – show your integrity by being on time and doing what you say you will do.

4. Loyalty – be loyal to those not present and defend them.

5. Tolerance – attribute good motives to others – avoid being biased or prejudiced.

6. Humility – recognize you don't have all the answers and insights – be teachable.

7. Accountability – be quick to apologize for mistakes and clear up misunderstandings.

8. Cooperation – abide by the rules and be generous to others.

9. Justice – strive to return kindness for offense, patience for impatience.

10. Communication – share ideas and reasons while maintaining genuine respect for others feelings.

Trust is gained more by our behavior or conduct than by our skill and words. We must trust others if we expect them to trust us. Here's a story that illustrates the point.

A well-known contractor worked for several years and was getting ready to retire. He had a fine reputation and had done well and was going to enjoy a leisurely retirement. In wrapping up his business, there were several things to finalize, so he had Jeff, an employee who had been with him for several years, finish a very recently started house that was to be sold. The contractor told Jeff how much money was available and when it was to be finished. Jeff started as usual, hard working and loyal, but after awhile he began to say to himself, "Why take so much pains on this job? The contractor will soon retire and will be gone and no one will know the difference."

Jeff began to leave out certain things that would not be readily noticed and justified himself by saying, "I will spend that extra time with my family." Next Jeff further justified himself by calling himself "practical," as he cut back on the insulation. He used fewer nails and cut many corners. As the sub-contractors worked, they seemed to sense that this project wasn't very important, so they also were more concerned with speed than quality. When the carpet layers came in, it was difficult because the house wasn't square, and nothing seemed to fit as it should. Even the doors would drift open if not closed tightly. When the house was finished, it looked good from the outside because of the paint and landscaped yard, but Jeff knew that it was vastly inferior.

To celebrate the end of a career, the contractor had his employees all over for dinner and they enjoyed a good evening. At the conclusion, the contractor expressed appreciation for their years of service and gave gifts to each one. To Jeff he said, "I appreciate all you've done for me. I felt certain you would enjoy building your own home." And he handed him the keys to the inferior house he had built.

During the building of the house, Jeff had used self-justification to save a little time or effort. Now, he had to live in the house of his own building. Many times in the future Jeff would be faced with the problems of his own making. We each have to live in the house we build. How much care do we put into it?

Chapter 16

Eight Vital Keys for Success in the Farrier Business

Chapter 16

Eight Vital Keys for Success in the Farrier Business

Eight Vital Keys

When I close my clinics on the business of horseshoeing, I often present what has come to be known as my "Eight Vital Keys" speech. It is a summary of the principles discussed in this book. I have received many letters and comments that prove to me that these principles are keys to changing one's life and farrier business. Good luck as you apply them!

1. Commit to Master Your Craft

You must love your work enough to commit to its mastery. Recognize there are no shortcuts. You must pay the price. Skill equals accuracy plus speed. Skill development takes time, but it is possible by everyone who applies themselves, breaks apart the skill process and patiently practices until it becomes a subconscious habit. Be persistent and determined to succeed.

Farriers as a group suffer from a lack of self-confidence. I believe that much of this feeling comes from lack of effort to really master their craft. You cannot honestly feel good about what you do until you can do it well. Self-confidence comes from seeing where you are and liking what you see. You cannot be happy and have real joy in your work until you master that work.

Set goals. Commit to pay the preparation price to achieve them. The will to prepare to win is more important than the will to win. One goal might be certification – but your goals should even be above and beyond that. Helping horses and their owners requires consistent commitment and creativity. When you stop getting better, you cease to be good at what you do.

Sure, it takes effort, focus and time to master traditional techniques, but when you do it, work becomes a pleasure. Then you can do better work, do it faster and have the satisfaction that comes from self-mastery and preserving a traditional skill.

2. Decide to Live with Integrity

What would you like others to say about you? What kind of legacy would you like to leave for your family and your clients? Would you like to be known as one who was true to his values and lived with integrity? Wouldn't that be a wonderful legacy to leave to your family? It would be more valuable than a large sum of money.

Competency equals skill plus character. Both are necessary. Just being a good person is great, but it is not enough. To be competent, you must also have skill. On the other hand, having skill without character is not valued, either. Many of these types of persons can be identified as con persons who are anxious to sell themselves and their products to an unsuspecting public.

The best people want to be the best. They want to be honest. Be honest and true to yourself. When you are dishonest, the person you cheat the most is yourself. I first heard the following poem from Gary Richins in a Franklin Covey time management seminar.

The Man in the Glass

*When you get what you want
in your struggle for self
And the world makes
you king for a day,*

*Just go to the mirror
and look at yourself
And see what that man
has to say.
For it isn't your father
or mother or wife
Whose judgment upon you
must pass.
The fellow whose verdict
counts most in your life
Is the one staring back
from the glass.*

*You may be like Jack Horner
and chisel a plum
And think you're a
wonderful guy.
But the man in the glass
says you're only a bum
If you can't look him
straight in the eye.
He's the fellow to please –
never mind all the rest,
For he's with you clear to the end.
And you've passed your most
dangerous, difficult test
If the man in the glass
is your friend.*

*You may fool the whole world
down the pathway of years
And get pats on the back
as you pass.
But your final reward
will be heartache and tears
If you've cheated the man
in the glass.*

Circumstances don't make people what they are; they only reveal their true nature. Gratitude is the hallmark of a noble soul. Be grateful and express it often to those who ride with you on the trails of life.

3. Read One-Half Hour Every Day

Read one-half hour every day, more if you can. Read in your field and related fields. Learn vocabulary. Share the experience and wisdom of others. I have done this for an hour or more each day – sometimes three or more hours, for many years. My goal has been at least a book a week. This has been a great blessing to my clients and me.

Some books and materials need to be read and reread. Our "knowledge buckets" have holes in them. We have to keep pouring water into them to keep them full. If we neglect pouring knowledge in, soon we will not know as much as we used to. Like the popular statement said around universities a few years ago, "If you graduated with an advanced degree five or more years ago, you *used* to know a lot!"

There is so much to keep up on. It is said that the knowledge in many fields is doubling every four years. We must keep up to be suc-

cessful. How much faith would you have in a doctor who had no books in his office and never read anything? What if he said, "I learned all I need to know in medical school 20 years ago. I just wing it every time." Would you feel comfortable with that? No! Chances are you would run if you heard a doctor say that! We expect to be treated with value by a trained professional. If we expect to be treated like a professional, we must act like one.

A few years ago, I was in Arizona presenting a clinic and met a man I hadn't seen for 35 years. I was glad to learn that he was still shoeing. He had been one of my teachers many years previously. But his attitude seemed to be one of, *I know it all, I don't need to learn anymore.* The local veterinarian told me this man was one of the worst shoers in the area. He was actually referred to as a "foot butcher." Why? He hadn't progressed. In fact, he had actually regressed. As the saying goes, he was "corrupted by his own company" and had ceased to learn.

Make it a practice to have new information to share with clients. Be up on current topics and know how to advise clients on the latest industry "fads" and issues. The

Reading warms up our minds like athletes warm up their bodies before competing.

more clients value your knowledge, the more they will value your services. By reading, we can learn information it has taken many lifetimes to learn. Reading warms up our minds like athletes warm up their bodies before competing. Don't neglect this valuable tool to help build your business.

Earl Nightingale, a famous radio personality of a few years ago, said, "An hour of study a day on a given subject can make anyone a foremost expert in that subject in five years."

Jim Rohn, one of the most compelling and inspirational speakers of our day, has said, "All the successful movers and shakers with whom I have had contact are good readers. Their curiosity drives them. They simply have to know. They constantly seek new ways to become better.

"All leaders are readers. Today we also learn through the miracle of electronic publishing—through audio and videotapes. Thousands of books and tapes tell us how to be a stronger, more decisive, effective leader and develop influence. Yet many do not use this wealth of knowledge. How do you explain that?

"Thousands of successful people have written and recorded

An hour of study a day on a given subject can make anyone a foremost expert in that subject in five years.

their inspiring stories. Yet some people don't want to read or listen. They say, 'I struggle home from work, eat, watch a little TV, go to bed. I can't stay up half the night and READ.' This is the sincere person who is behind on the bills. You can work hard and be sincere all of your life and still wind up broke, confused and embarrassed."

Devote just 30 minutes a day to learning. You want to really do well? Stretch your 30 minutes. All of us can afford to miss a few meals; none can afford to lose out on ideas, examples and inspiration. Don't miss learning. Think of your reading time as "tapping the treasure of ideas." You are what you read.

4. Listen To Audio Tapes While Driving

Audiotapes are not used effectively by most farriers. They should be. We have great opportunity to profit from them. Good collections of audio learning tapes are available in any public library. But you must believe they can make a difference and be willing to sacrifice listening to music while you drive. Listen to music while you work. But, listen to audio learning tapes while you drive.

Farriers drive approximately 25,000 miles per year. At 50 miles an hour, this equals 500 hours of time in the truck. This is the same number of hours in a college semester. Turn your truck into a rolling university by listening as you travel. If you charge mileage for travel, you can even get paid for learning!

Listening to tapes makes us more capable and competent. We exercise our minds by visualizing what is being discussed. We are more interesting to talk to and attractive to clients. Often, just one idea will make the difference in your life or in someone else's.

I know a farrier from Texas who set a goal to pass the AFA Journeyman farrier exam. He had a difficult challenge with reading because of a limited opportunity for schooling. So he had his wife read selected sections of my book *Principles of Horseshoeing II* into a tape recorder, then he "overlearned" those chapters on anatomy by playing the tapes over and over as he traveled to his appointments in remote rural areas. Then he would have his wife ask him questions to test his knowledge. Soon, he had mastered the anatomy terms that were once so difficult for him. His fear was replaced by confidence.

Another farrier from the Eastern seaboard reported using my audio learning tapes to help him win over an important client. While on the way to the appointment, he happened to be listening to a piece I had prepared on the uses of pads. As soon as he arrived, the potential long-term client asked him a question about pads. He briefly outlined the contents of the tape that was fresh on his mind. The person was so impressed, she hired him to do a large account that meant a significant increase in his business' bottom line.

5. Make Good Use of Your Time

Time is your most valuable business asset. Abraham Lincoln said, "A lawyer's time is his stock and trade." This is true of any professional, and especially the farrier and veterinarian. Time is our most valuable business asset.

Spend your time developing your strengths. Avoid dwelling on weaknesses. Hire people to support you instead of expending energy on deficient areas. Recognize the greater contribution you can make by focusing on your strengths. The highest levels of achievement come when people are matched with work that they like. Studies at Stanford University show that exceptional intelligence doesn't guarantee extraordinary accomplishment. Instead, spectacular achievers are those who are focused on what they really want to do in life.

How do you use your time? Ralph Waldo Emerson said, "Of what use would immortality be to someone who could not use well one-half hour?" How are you managing the time you have right now? Are you capable of working effectively on your own? Corporate studies show that only 2% of people are capable of working without supervision. Are you?

Part of time management is a good time management system that helps you "organize and execute around priorities." This can be as simple as a pocket day planner or as involved as an elaborate software program.

Practice timing your work with a clock on the job. Practice until you can accurately predict how long it takes to do each part of the job. Work toward goals to reduce that time. Constant clock watching to compete against yourself makes you more efficient. Since horseshoeing is piecework, it pays to be as efficient as you can.

Daily practice is necessary to achieve mastery. Practice at home first making shoes or other skills that may be awkward or less than impressive, not in front of clients. Otherwise, you may lose their confidence, as well as your own.

Kids and spouses spell love only one way, T-I-M-E.

Avoid coffee breaks or lunches during the day. Eat and rest in the truck between stops. You can add as much as two months of income to your bottom line if you skip coffee breaks and lunch breaks. Of course, exceptions are when you can use that time to advantage to network with people who can help you build your business.

Try to get your appointment and phone work done during the day, either by yourself or by hiring an experienced home office secretary to take calls, schedule appointments and reminders, even do your books. Design a system to relieve yourself of the responsibility of making calls in the evening after coming home from a busy day of shoeing.

Schedule and spend quality *and* quantity time with your family. Kids and spouses spell love only one way, T-I-M-E.

6. Be Professional

Presenting a professional image does more than any of us realize to influence the clients' opinions of us and determine the position we occupy in their minds. Dress appropriately; wear clean and workmanlike clothes that don't call attention to yourself. Clothing should fit so cleavages are covered for both men and women. Exposure while working is distracting and even offensive to many. When you get sweaty and dirty, change your shirt and wash up so you give a good appearance at the next appointment.

Pay attention to grooming. Brush your teeth. Use breath mints. Men should shave daily. Avoid wearing and showing off costly jewelry or clothes on the job. Get a haircut regularly. As success trainer Brian Tracy says, "Your income will go up as your hairline goes up." If you wear long hair, have it styled or put up under your cap. Long hair can be a safety issue, as well as an income liability, in horseshoeing.

Speak clearly and cleanly. Get a reputation as someone who can be trusted to do the right thing. Make people glad to be around you by informing them and laughing with them. Be sensitive to the client's feelings and attitudes. Display a positive, interested and caring attitude. Work on your vocabulary by reading and listening to tapes so you can serve a "banquet" of words when you speak, not fast and often indigestible food.

Keep your bad habits to yourself. Unhealthy choices aren't as popular today as they were a few years ago. For example, more than 65% of our customers don't use tobacco. It is offensive to them if you do. Many clients have children and they are concerned that you have a positive influence on them. If you use tobacco, consider giving it up, or at the very least, use it in the truck between appointments when you are not in the presence of the clients or their children. Using it shows more than an ignorance of the health issues; it shows insensitivity to the clients' cares and concerns.

Practice safety. It shows consideration for yourself and your clients. Take off watches and rings when you work. Wear safety shoes to prevent broken toes. Wear safety glasses, especially when using power tools and forging. Wear ear protection. Cotton clothing is safest around the forge fire. Carry a fire extinguisher. Protect yourself and bystanders from possible injury from grinding sparks and welding glare. Your attitude of safety shows consideration for everyone. Cleaning up after the job is polite and shows consideration.

Treat clients like they are worth a lot to you. They are, when you figure their value over time. A happy client will finance your lifestyle over the years of your career. They are "partners" in help-

Be sensitive to the client's feelings and attitudes. Display a positive, interested and caring attitude.

ing you provide for your family. Clients must continually be sold on the value of your experience and service to them. Telling someone you appreciate them once isn't as effective as repeating it regularly, even daily.

7. Follow the Leaders

Identify the leaders in the industry. Look to those who are doing what you want to do and being what you want to be, then follow them. Your reference group will encourage or hinder your progress. See yourself as identifying with the leaders. Hang around them, go to clinics conducted by them. Use materials and tools designed by them. Imitate their style until you develop your own.

Pay any price to get the information and motivation from the best. Study how they do it. Imitate and practice until you can do it. Dedicate yourself to a schedule of rote practice until you can do what they do. Take every opportunity to get near them and learn their secrets of success. If you can't find one who has all of his or her life together, imitate the best traits from each of several, making them part of your work and life.

One of the big problems in the farrier industry is that so many farriers are getting a bad start by learning from people who are not leaders. Many "ride along" with those folks who can't do the job correctly themselves. These are the wrong people to learn from. Choose true leaders for your mentors. Do what you see them do. Listen and apply the advice they give. The best pay dedicated teachers can receive is seeing their students be enthusiastic about the craft they love.

The best pay dedicated teachers can receive is seeing their students be enthusiastic about the craft they love.

After you get where you want to go, become a leader yourself and others will look to you. Become a trusted example and pass it on.

Our entire lives are influenced by what we know and what we do. Our awareness often determines our performance. High awareness multiplied by high performance equals mastery. If we learn only methods, we'll be tied to them. But if we learn the principles behind the methods, we can devise our own methods to fit any situation.

The person who knows *how* will have a job; the person who knows *why* will be the boss. *How* is the process or method. *Why* is the purpose or principle. Develop business systems based on principles. Ask yourself, "How would the person I would like to be most like do the things I'm about to do?"

8. Work Hard and Work Smart

To be successful, you must first believe you can. Then, you must work hard and work smart. Understand what Earl Nightingale called "the strangest secret in the world." That is, you become what you think about. You get what you expect. Your greatest limitation is your thinking – *stinkin' thinkin'* – as Zig Ziglar, author of *See You At The Top*, calls it.

In 1986, I earned a spot on the North American Horseshoeing Team. We held several clinics and practices. One was at the Budweiser Clydesdale Breeding Farm in St. Louis, Missouri. After the clinic and practice, we toured the Grant's Farm Zoo. They had some elephants there, and we struck up a conversation with the elephant trainer. We asked him how he trained the elephants. He taught us the importance of perception and reminded us of the power of habits formed in our minds.

He told us he ties up a baby elephant with a heavy log chain, then leads (drags) it with his Bigfoot 4x4 truck. He ties it down with a heavy chain where there is no escaping. He intimidates, even punishes the elephant to make it mad. The baby struggles with all its might, it bellows, it cries, it tries with all its might to free itself. It cannot. Then he reinforces this lesson using progressively smaller chains until it is full-grown. When the elephants are adults, five to six tons in weight, some of the strongest beasts on earth, they can be tied with a small chain no larger than one you would use to tie a large dog. The elephant has become a prisoner of its own mind. It doesn't just believe, it *knows*, and it is SURE it cannot get away.

We are often prisoners of our beliefs and perceptions. Our mind is made up about what is truth or untruth. We can turn obstacles into opportunities. But we must change our minds before we can progress and move up to a new level.

Which statements describe your mindset?

Obstacles – Untruths	Opportunities – Truths
Our abilities are genetic and unchangeable.	Our underdeveloped potential is huge.
Our school curriculum is designed to assure success.	Our school system discriminates against creativity.
Our beliefs and perceptions are the only ones that will work.	Our beliefs and perceptions can greatly enhance or limit us.

Don't let what you cannot do prevent you from doing what you can do.

Some say that farriers are slow learners. It is true that it may take years for some of us to realize that we have no talent for this business. But, by then, we're making so much money, we can't afford to quit!

Getting your business up and running is like flying an airplane. Most of the energy and power necessary to make the trip is expended when overcoming inertia and making the takeoff. You don't have to be good to start, but you have to start to be good! Get going!

Appendix 1

Self-Assessment Attitude Test
For Aspiring Farriers

 *Appendix 1*

Self-Assessment Attitude Test For Aspiring Farriers

The following attitude test is for horseshoers. There are no right or wrong answers; each has a specified point value. Total your points at the end to see how you measure up.

1. How do you feel about hard work?
   a. I can't work long hours.
   b. I do what the job requires.
   c. I have a proven history of being a hard worker.
   d. I can work hard if I have to, but would rather not.

2. How would you characterize your approach to life?
   a. I like to know what is expected of me.
   b. I hate to have someone peering over my shoulder.
   c. I prefer to have explicit instructions. If I'm not asked to do something, it won't get done.
   d. I'm a self-starter and will be my best every time.

3. How does your personality affect the way you feel about work?
   a. I have to see projects through to their completion.
   b. Sometimes I drop out.
   c. I am determined and stick to the task like a fly on flypaper.
   d. I am an easygoing person.

4. What do you depend on when making an assessment/evaluation of a horse?
   a. I'm really smart.
   b. I follow my gut instinct.
   c. I am decisive.
   d. I have experience.

5. How do you feel about working with or relying on others?
    a. I'm reliable and find others to be the same.
    b. I'm careful not to over-promise.
    c. I'm very results-oriented.
    d. Nice guys finish last.

6. How would you describe your energy level?
    a. My health is OK.
    b. Nothing can wear me out.
    c. I have enough stamina.
    d. I need time off.

7. How do you feel about doing something you've never done before?
    a. I do a lot of research, but rarely do anything.
    b. I am very timid about new things.
    c. I dive in headfirst.
    d. I bet on my own skills, not on luck.

8. When you step back and think about where you are going, you realize that:
    a. My most important job is setting meaningful goals.
    b. I don't know what "success" means.
    c. I want to make enough money to retire comfortably.
    d. I get bored when things go smoothly.

9. How would you describe your communication skills?
    a. I always communicate clearly to veterinarians, horse owners and other farriers.
    b. I sometimes have trouble getting my point across.
    c. I tell others what to do; it's up to them to do it.
    d. I'm a doer, not a communicator.

10. When I get home from a long day of shoeing horses:
    a. I put off doing accounting and paper work and watch television instead.
    b. I read and study to improve myself.
    c. I go right to sleep.
    d. I review the day's work, set goals to improve and work on one more thing to improve myself before going to sleep.

11. When you find yourself in a situation where issues are unresolved, how do you respond?
    a. I withdraw and refuse to talk with others.
    b. I get stressed out if I don't know the answer.
    c. I can live with incomplete information and uncertainty.
    d. I can't always wait for complete information before making a decision.

12. When the treatment you use to help a horse doesn't work and the horse dies, how do you respond?
    a. I wonder if I should stay in horseshoeing.
    b. I blame the veterinarian or the horse owner for incompetent care.
    c. I roll with the punches and try to help the next horse.
    d. I find that I have lost confidence in my ability to treat any horse.

13. How do you feel about the farrier business?
    a. This business really excites me.
    b. I see this business as my ticket to wealth and riches.
    c. The more I know about this business, the more I like it.
    d. There are plenty of exciting businesses. The trick is focusing on one of them.

14. How do you feel when something has gone wrong and the responsibility of a case rests with you?
    a. I don't make excuses.
    b. Unfair competition scares me.
    c. I learn from my mistakes.
    d. I'd rather be a leader than a follower.

15. How do you feel about other farriers in your association?
    a. I do my work and let them go on with theirs.
    b. I tell people what to do, rather than work with others.
    c. I welcome responsibility.
    d. I work well with others.

16. How confident are you that you will succeed in the farrier business?
    a. I feel "I can do it" most of the time.
    b. Nothing will stop me, and I will keep on trucking.
    c. I sometimes wonder if I'm making the right decision.
    d. If it doesn't work out, I'll try something else.

17. How do you feel about playing all of the roles in your farrier business?
    a. I have all the business skills I need.
    b. I'm a people person. What else do I need?
    c. I don't know what I need to know. Help!
    d. I have most of the skills I need, and know how to find people with those I lack.

18. How do you feel about telling others you are getting into the farrier business?
    a. I'm keeping my business a secret right now.
    b. My friends and family are behind me.
    c. My spouse is worried about the risk, but we'll work it out.
    d. I don't know if my friends and family think it is a good idea.

19. What do you think of creativity and change?
    a. I like to follow a set pattern of guidelines or rules.
    b. Being innovative and creative is a drawback in farriery.
    c. I like to come up with new solutions to problems.
    d. Once my plans are set, I never deviate from them.

20. How do you feel when another farrier critiques your work?
    a. I set goals so I can measure my progress.
    b. I can do it better than they can anyway.
    c. I welcome constructive criticism.
    d. I want to hear what others have to say – it is very important to me.

21. When you shape a keg shoe:
    a. I make many trips back and forth between the anvil and the horse.
    b. I have a good image of the shape of the foot in my mind and can shape the shoe so it fits right the first time.
    c. I have trouble "seeing" or locking onto the image of the horse's foot.
    d. It takes forever to get the shoe level.

22. When a horse acts up and nearly kills you, how do you respond?
    a. I refuse to continue my work and leave.
    b. I hit the horse with my rasp or whatever tool I have in my hand.
    c. I swear at the owner and the horse (including reciting its pedigree).
    d. I ask the owner if he would like me to train the horse.

23. When presented with an opportunity to attend a farrier training clinic or seminar:
    a. I'll only go if it is free.
    b. I pay whatever price necessary to learn from those I know can teach me.
    c. I stay at home and read a book or magazine instead.
    d. I only go if my competitors are going.

Scoring the Self-Assessment Attitude Test

Determine your score by giving yourself the following number of points for each answer you've chosen.

1. Work Ethic
   a. 0   b. 2   c. 5   d. 3
2. Self-Starter
   a. 3   b. 0   c. 1   d. 5
3. Commitment
   a. 3   b. 1   c. 5   d. 1
4. Good Judgment
   a. 0   b. 2   c. 3   d. 5
5. Reliability
   a. 5   b. 2   c. 3   d. 0
6. Enthusiasm
   a. 2   b. 5   c. 3   d. 2
7. Moderate Risk Taker
   a. 1   b. 1   c. 3   d. 5
8. Sense of Achievement
   a. 5   b. 0   c. 2   d. 4
9. Communication Skills
   a. 5   b. 2   c. 3   d. 0
10. Discipline
    a. 0   b. 4   c. 1   d. 5
11. Physical Toughness
    a. 2   b. 0   c. 3   d. 5

12. Mental Toughness
    a. 2   b. 1   c. 5   d. 0
13. Passion/Desire
    a. 5   b. 0   c. 4   d. 5
14. Responsibility
    a. 2   b. 0   c. 3   d. 5
15. Farrier Liaison
    a. 2   b. 1   c. 3   d. 5
16. Self-Confidence
    a. 3   b. 5   c. 2   d. 0
17. Management Skills
    a. 0   b. 0   c. 3   d. 5
18. Supportive Peer Group
    a. 0   b. 5   c. 5   d. 2
19. Creative and Innovative
    a. 0   b. 0   c. 5   d. 1
20. Teachable
    a. 5   b. 0   c. 3   d. 4
21. Visual Thinking Skills
    a. 0   b. 5   c. 2   d. 1
22. Patience/Temperament
    a. 3   b. 0   c. 0   d. 5
23. Knowledge Seeker
    a. 0   b. 5   c. 2   d. 1

Key to Your Score

- Your score can range from 0 to 115. These are indicators, not conclusive evidence that you should or should not get into the farrier business.

- A score of 90 or better indicates that you probably would do well in the farrier business.

- A score between 40 and 89 indicates that you should

think carefully about beginning a career in farriery.

- A score below 40 indicates that you should consider another career for the time-being.

Characteristics Important for Farriers to Possess

1. Work ethic

To be successful in the farrier business, you must have a strong work ethic. Not only do you need to have the drive to put in the hours to learn the craft and get good at it, you must also have the physical ability to survive in this demanding field. Some of the best success stories in the field come from those who have developed a strong work ethic from childhood.

2. Self-starter

To successfully master farriery, you must understand what motivates you. What will help you get going in the morning when your body hurts from the previous day's work? Understanding your motivation will give you the capacity to grow and improve. A good teacher can enhance the process, but if you always have to look to others for help in being motivated, you will never achieve the highest realms of success. Your quest for excellence in developing and mastering the skills of a highly effective farrier must be an integral part of what drives you. The principles, techniques and skills of developing a profitable farrier business will be of little value to you unless you have the motivation, discipline and commitment necessary to implement them in your life.

3. Commitment

Your level of commitment to succeed is a conscious choice that you must make. It takes discipline and dedication to endure the challenges that follow, once you make the commitment decision. Success in farriery will never be achieved until *you* make a serious personal commitment. No one else can do that for you. Perfecting farrier skills takes continuous motivation and dedicated practice over a period of years.

4. Good judgment

Good judgment is the ability to *apply* the lessons we learn from our experience. There is simply no substitute for experience. Reading and studying will never give a person the skill that can be learned in a short time while actually doing the work. A person with experience is considerably more productive than an inexperienced person. Everyone makes mistakes, but the experienced person learns life's lessons from their mistakes. Great educators have always recognized that we learn by doing.

5. Reliability

The *American Farriers Journal* in 1993 reported a survey of 318 horse owners. It indicates horse owners switch to another farrier due to failure to keep appointments and failure to return calls in a timely manner. In other words, horse owners demand reliability. Reliability is equated with integrity. Integrity is highly valued.

6. Enthusiasm

Enthusiasm is contagious. People like to be around someone who loves their work and loves life. It is largely a function of attitude.

7. Moderate risk taker

Being in business and investing in the tools, training and inventory necessary to succeed involves risk. The risk should be calculated, but it must be taken.

8. Sense of achievement

As you apply principles and improve in skill, you will progress from one level to the next. This progression, or movement, is what constitutes achievement. Achievement is a measurement of what you have accomplished. Your dreams become realities as you pay the price to progress.

9. Communication skills

Be courteous, direct and ask for feedback to determine if your communications are understood. Use simple analogies or metaphors when trying to express complete ideas.

10. Discipline

Success is only achieved by dedication and self-discipline. Discipline requires self-denial and routine scheduling. Disciplining your tongue and moods is critical.

11. Physical toughness

Farriers must develop tolerance to pain in order to survive this work. The physical stamina needed comes from being physically fit and is a critical key to success.

12. Mental toughness

Clients are emotionally involved with their horses and may not be as patient as you would like. Having emotional endurance will help you tolerate difficult horses and people.

13. Passion/desire

The most successful individuals in any field of endeavor are excited about their work. What they do gives meaning to their lives. Confucius said, "Choose the work you love, and you will never have to work a day in your life." Work will be enjoyable.

14. Responsibility

No one else but you can take responsibility for your personal growth. An independent, responsible person will be better able to work with other professionals in an interdependent relationship to arrive at the best solution.

15. Farrier liaison

Seek to gain support and advice from other farriers. Set an example in your relationships with others and your quest for knowledge.

16. Self-confidence

This is the fruit of taking responsibility for your life. Childhood experiences influence our ability to have confidence. These early influences can be overcome only with great effort.

17. Management skills

Take courses to improve your skills. Learn where to get help. Pay for specialists to help you get where you want to be.

18. Supportive peer group

We all hope that our closest associates and family members will support us and give positive feedback. We must decide what influence their input will have on us. Our level of commitment and priorities are often tested here. We may be strengthened or weakened by this influence.

19. Creative and innovative

Always look for a solution. Try to think out of the box. Consider as many alternatives as possible. Apply what you learn from other fields to farrier problems.

20. Teachable

Those who achieve the most in this profession are those who set goals to measure their progress, then accept advice from a coach or mentor who can help them analyze and improve their work to get more efficient results. To be teachable means implementing the recommendations and guidance of those who have gone before. They often know how to get from where you are to where you want to be with the least amount of trial and error.

21. Visual thinking skills

Successful farriers have the ability to visualize their success. You must see yourself achieving excellence in your mind before you will achieve excellence at the anvil or under the horse. Your mind will guide your actions toward the visualized goal.

22. Patience/temperament

Farriers must be patient with horses and people. Patience is self-control gained through discipline and practice. It is a virtue that is becoming rare in our society. The effort you make to develop it will pay big dividends.

23. Knowledge seeker

Realize you can never know all there is to know about your profession. Never be satisfied with your present level. Be committed to lifelong learning.

Identifying Your Aptitudes and Attitudes

Horseshoeing requires the ability to visualize and describe foot conditions to horse owners and veterinarians. You must learn technical vocabulary terms and be well read in your field. You must be able to write and illustrate clearly, calculate and write out the bills.

The following exercises will help you understand your aptitudes and attitudes.

   a. Earn a high school diploma or equivalent GED. More education is desirable. Courses in welding and small business management are especially valuable.

   b. Write a 75-to-100-word essay in your own handwriting demonstrating your ability to organize and express your thoughts on the subject "Why Horseshoeing Is My Career Choice." Communicate your passion for the subject in your essay.

c. List a profile of an ideal horseshoeing student. Explain why you do or do not fit each part of the profile.

Draw (do not trace) a mid-sagittal cross-section of a trimmed foot from memory and label the parts. The drawing must be the size of a number 0 shoe, or 11-inch foot. Neatness, proportion and color are important.

Appendix 2

Self-Assessment Physical Test
For Aspiring Farriers

 *Appendix 2*

Self-Assessment Physical Test For Aspiring Farriers

A principal factor that prevents persons from succeeding as farriers is physical fitness for the work. Horseshoeing is a physically demanding work requiring muscular strength, manual dexterity, horsemanship, hand/eye coordination and mental concentration. The ability to earn a living, as well as the ability to learn marketable skills will be severely limited if one is not fit for this work. Physical preparation for farrier work is highly recommended. The following tests will demonstrate to you and your mentor that you are qualified by your aptitude and preparation to do this work.

1. What is your physical condition? Get a doctor to determine your level of physical fitness, checking to determine if the following areas are free from debilitating conditions.

    a. Knees   ☐ Pass   ☐ Fail
    b. Wrists   ☐ Pass   ☐ Fail
    c. Back   ☐ Pass   ☐ Fail
    d. Hands   ☐ Pass   ☐ Fail
    e. Hernia   ☐ Pass   ☐ Fail
    f. Respiratory   ☐ Pass   ☐ Fail
    g. Heart   ☐ Pass   ☐ Fail

2. What is your strength and fitness to begin farrier work? You should work up to these minimums before beginning farrier work.

    a. Lift a 100 lb. (or more) anvil or weight from ground level onto the tailgate of a pickup truck. Repeat twice.

    ☐ Pass   ☐ Fail

    b. Do 30 situps with knees flat and hands behind head in 2 minutes.

    ☐ Pass   ☐ Fail

c. Do 30 pushups from hands while resting on toes with body straight in 1 minute.

☐ Pass ☐ Fail

d. Do 5 chinups with hands facing forward or backward in 30 seconds.

☐ Pass ☐ Fail

e. Run a mile in 7 minutes.

☐ Pass ☐ Fail

f. Touch tips of fingers (or palms of hands) on ground with knees straight.

☐ Pass ☐ Fail

g. Do 10 knee bends alternating right/left leg, hands behind head in 20 seconds.

☐ Pass ☐ Fail

h. Do 10 squeezing exercise repetitions with a heavy hand exerciser, or squeeze a bathroom scale with both hands to 80 pounds at least 5 times. Work toward the goal of 100 to 150 pounds.

☐ Pass ☐ Fail

3. Demonstrate strength and dexterity with tools by:

a. Driving 8 #5 horseshoe nails flush into a board in 45 seconds.

☐ Pass ☐ Fail

b. Rapidly cutting a 6-inch distance of 1/2 inch plastic horseshoe pad with hoof nippers.

☐ Pass ☐ Fail

c. Rasping the end of a plastic well casing pipe, or a 4"x4" wooden post, level with a hoof rasp.

☐ Pass ☐ Fail

d. Concaving or seating out the inside foot surface of a horseshoe, and level it with overlapping hammer blows.

☐ Pass ☐ Fail

e. Straightening a heated keg shoe using forging tools.

☐ Pass   ☐ Fail

f. Forging one end of the straight bar made from a keg shoe square to a point and forging the other end round to a point.

☐ Pass   ☐ Fail

g. Finishing the heels of a keg shoe by hot rasping-safeing the ground side and boxing the foot side.

☐ Pass   ☐ Fail

h. Bending a heated keg shoe into a circle shape and one into a diamond shape using a forge, hammer, tongs and anvil.

☐ Pass   ☐ Fail

4. Assess your ability to humanely care for a horse.

a. Catch

☐ Pass   ☐ Fail

b. Groom

☐ Pass   ☐ Fail

c. Feed

☐ Pass   ☐ Fail

d. De-worm

☐ Pass   ☐ Fail

e. Immunize

☐ Pass   ☐ Fail

5. Assess your ability to tie the following knots, or apply the restraint techniques in an effective and humane manner.

a. Tying a halter hitch

☐ Pass   ☐ Fail

b. Tying a bowline

☐ Pass   ☐ Fail

   c. Tying two half-hitches

      ☐ Pass   ☐ Fail

   d. Using a scotch hobble rope

      ☐ Pass   ☐ Fail

   e. Using a front leg hobble strap

      ☐ Pass   ☐ Fail

   f. Using a lip chain

      ☐ Pass   ☐ Fail

   g. Using a nose twitch

      ☐ Pass   ☐ Fail

6. Assess your ability to cue and ride a horse at all its natural gaits. A 10 is capable; a 0 is not capable. Rating (1-10) _____

7. Assess your ability to hold up the horse's feet in the shoeing position for a period of up to 2 hours. A 10 is capable; a 0 is not capable. Rating (1-10) _____

Appendix 3

Questions For Levels – Subject Areas

Appendix 3

Questions For Levels – Subject Areas

STUDENT/ APPRENTICE	BEGINNING	WORKING	ADVANCED
Capable Helper	Skilled Farrier	Competent Farrier	Respected Professional
Horse Understanding	**Foot Understanding**	**Leg Understanding**	**Limb Understanding**
Bone – common names	Bone–scientific names	Leg structure/function	Limb tendon function
Hoof structures	Foot sensitive structures	Blood pumping mechanism	Limb ligament function
Hoof functions	Foot elastic structures	Leg tendons	Blood circulation
Head restraints	Horse conformation	Leg ligaments	Nervation
Working positions	Conformation consequences	Behavior	Medical terms
Shoeing sequence	Training for shoeing	Physiology	Pathology – foot
Leg unsoundnesses	Leg restraints	Normal gaits	Pathology – leg
Shoe types and sizes	Shoe shapes	Gait defects	Shoe types and uses
Nail types and sizes	Shoe styles and uses	Shoe applications	Veterinary protocol
Oxy-acetylene safety	Keg shoe alterations	Shoe making	Radiograph reading
Arc welding safety	Forge safety	Forge welding	Alternate therapies
A bony growth or abnormal bump in side of hock is called *bone spavin.*	Severe cow hocks can predispose a horse to *bone spavin.*	A horse that moves short behind and wears out the front toe of its shoes may have *bone spavin.*	An exostosis on inside of tarsus near cunean tendon can be treated mechanically with this shoe – *graduated, wedge heeled shoe or spavin shoe.*

STUDENT/APPRENTICE LEVEL

Sample Questions

1. When viewed from the side, the position of the horse's hind leg when held in a comfortable position for shoeing can best be described as:
   a. the cannon bone is perpendicular to the ground
   b. the long pastern bone is parallel to the ground
   c. the cannon bone is parallel to the ground
   d. the long pastern bone is perpendicular to the ground

2. Bones in the horse's foot are:
   a. cannon, coffin
   b. coffin, short pastern
   c. navicular, long pastern
   d. cannon, navicular

3. The portion of the hoof anatomically and physiologically designed to bear the most weight is:
   a. sole
   b. apex of frog
   c. wall
   d. periople

4. The moisture content of healthy hoof parts is approximately:
   a. wall – 25%, sole – 50%, frog – 25%
   b. sole – 33%, wall – 23%, frog – 43%
   c. frog – 75%, sole – 25%, wall – 50%
   d. wall – 25%, frog – 50%, sole – 75%

5. A round-shaped front foot that measures 4 3/4″ across at its widest point will require this size shoe if it ends at the buttresses:
   a. 000
   b. 00
   c. 0
   d. 1

6. Nails that would accurately fit in a #0 rim shoe:
   a. #3 regular head or 4 city head
   b. #5 city head or MX 50
   c. #5 regular head or MX 60
   d. #7 city head or MX 70

7. Ringbone is located around which bone?
   a. cannon
   b. sesamoid
   c. pastern
   d. navicular

8. Bowed tendons are the most common leg injury causing a horse to retire from racing. What tendon is most commonly involved?
   a. common extensor tendon
   b. lateral extensor tendon
   c. superficial flexor tendon
   d. deep flexor tendon

9. Osselets occur at this joint:
   a. coffin
   b. pastern
   c. navicular
   d. fetlock

10. Oxy-acetylene tanks must be firmly secured, and the valves protected for maximum safety in this position in your truck:
    a. vertical – valve up
    b. 45° angle
    c. horizontal
    d. vertical – valve down

11. Visible splints on the inside of the cannon region are usually considered:
    a. evidence of a shoeing error
    b. an unsoundness
    c. a blemish
    d. a lameness

12. Pressing on the tops of the lateral cartilages to check their flexibility is a test for:
    a. navicular
    b. ringbone
    c. sesamoiditis
    d. sidebone

BEGINNING FARRIER LEVEL

Sample Questions

1. How many functioning sesamoids are in the horse's leg below the knee?
   a. none
   b. one
   c. two
   d. three

2. The scientific name of the lateral splint bone of the hind leg is:
   a. fourth metatarsal
   b. third metatarsal
   c. second metatarsal
   d. second metacarpal

3. The primary function of the laminae in the horse's foot is to:
   a. absorb most of the concussion
   b. pump blood
   c. suspend bone column from hoof capsule
   d. supply blood to the frog

4. The amount of each alar or lateral cartilage contained within the hoof capsule is:
   a. approximately one-half
   b. approximately one-fourth
   c. approximately all
   d. none

5. The extensor process of the distal phalanx is in close proximity to:
   a. the lateral extensor tendon
   b. the lateral cartilages
   c. the digital cushion
   d. the coronary cushion

6. Conformation of the horse that will most likely cause limb interference at the trot is:
   a. toed-in
   b. toed-out
   c. base narrow
   d. club feet

7. Conformations that predispose a horse to forging:
   a. long back, short legs
   b. long back, long legs
   c. short back, short legs
   d. short back, long legs

8. Normally, nails should be placed in the front half of the shoe because:
   a. the wall is always thicker in the quarters
   b. the rear of the hoof wall moves as it bears weight
   c. the hoof wall makes a greater angle at the toe
   d. more secure nailing is possible at the toe

9. A function of clips is to:
   a. take stress off the nails
   b. increase shoe wear
   c. decrease shoe weight
   d. increase traction

10. A function of bar shoes is to:
    a. take stress off the nails
    b. stabilize the shoe on the foot
    c. transfer weight bearing
    d. increase shoe wear

11. What precautions should be taken if you accidentally quick a horse?
    a. remove the nail on each side of the wound
    b. dip the foot in cold water and apply a wedge pad
    c. alert the owner and ask about current tetanus immunization
    d. remove the shoes

12. The center of gravity is a useful aid in dressing feet and fitting shoes. Where is it located when viewing the bottom of the foot?
    a. the apex of the untrimmed frog
    b. about 1 ¹/₂″ inches in front of the frog
    c. at the widest point of the frog
    d. about 3/8 inch to ¹/₂″ inch behind the apex of the trimmed frog.

13. A horse that is trained for shoeing should:
    a. stand still and balance on three legs
    b. be kind to other horses
    c. be pretty to see
    d. be nice to ride

WORKING FARRIER LEVEL

Sample Questions

1. The following structures are *not* in the horse's foot:
   a. proximal annular ligament, superficial flexor tendon
   b. distal annular ligament, deep flexor tendon
   c. common extensor tendon, suspensory ligament
   d. collateral ligaments, impar ligament

2. Cross-firing is a fault of gait that normally occurs at the:
   a. walk
   b. trot
   c. pace
   d. canter

3. Name a three-beat gait:
   a. walk
   b. trot
   c. pace
   d. canter

4. Horses are able to rest standing up due to the presence of a:
   a. hock-joint lock
   b. reciprocal and stay apparatus
   c. third eyelid
   d. cecum

5. The check ligament of the deep flexor tendon in the hind limb is:
   a. above the hock joint
   b. below the fetlock joint
   c. above the knee joint
   d. below the hock joint

6. The check ligament of the superficial flexor tendon in the front limb is:
   a. above the knee joint
   b. below the fetlock joint
   c. below the knee joint
   d. above the hock joint

7. The suspensory ligament of the navicular bone or the collateral ligament of the navicular bone attaches to the bone at its:
   a. proximal border
   b. distal border
   c. flexor surface
   d. joint surface

8. The hoof normally grows at the rate of approximately:
   a. one inch per year
   b. one inch per month
   c. 3/8 inch per month
   d. 1/4 inch per week

9. Most venous blood is pumped from the foot by the:
   a. downward movement of the pastern
   b. upward movement of the frog
   c. compression of the hoof wall
   d. valves in the foot arteries

10. Fullering is put in horseshoes to:
    a. stop the foot from sliding
    b. increase weight by filling with dirt
    c. increase traction by filling with dirt
    d. make the foot breakover

11. The hoof wall is partially composed of hoof tubules. They increase in diameter as you go from:
    a. proximal to distal
    b. distal to proximal
    c. inside to outside
    d. outside to inside

12. The ends of the hoof tester are in closest proximity to the ends of the navicular bone when located approximately at:
    a. The widest part of the hoof one inch below the coronary band
    b. The middle of the rear third of the hoof midway between the coronary band and the ground
    c. One-half inch forward from the widest part of the frog and one-half inch down from the coronary band
    d. The widest part of the hoof one-half inch below the coronary band

ADVANCED FARRIER LEVEL

Sample Questions

1. A lateral medial radiograph taken at mid-hoof level of a normal foot trimmed in three-dimensional balance will show the distal border of the distal phalanx at approximately this angle:
   a. 5° below horizontal
   b. 15° above horizontal
   c. 10° above horizontal
   d. parallel to the hoof base

2. The sole receives the majority of its blood supply from:
   a. the circumflex artery of the distal phalanx
   b. the paracuneal artery
   c. branches of the coroneal artery
   d. branches of the digital artery coming through the bottom of the distal phalanx

3. The artery that may be compromised by a tongue on a frog support or heart bar shoe that doesn't correspond to the shape of the frog is:
   a. the circumflex artery of the distal phalanx
   b. the paracuneal artery
   c. branches of the coroneal artery
   d. branches of the distal artery coming through the bottom of the distal phalanx

4. The major blood supply for the navicular bone comes through the:
   a. lateral cartilages
   b. deep flexor tendons
   c. collateral and impar ligaments
   d. distal annular ligaments

5. The palmar or posterior digital nerve supplies sensation to these areas:
   a. coronary and front pastern
   b. rear pastern and coronary
   c. navicular and upper laminar
   d. sole and navicular

6. The most effective treatment for navicular disease according to *The Manual of Equine Practice* by Dr. Reuben Rose and Dr. David Hodgson of Australia is:
   a. radiographs and heart bars
   b. egg bars and isoxiprine
   c. egg bars and side clips
   d. square toe with calks

7. The most effective shoe for chronic laminitis according to Dr. Robert Eustace, the University of Bristol, England, in his book, *Explaining Laminitis and Its Prevention* is:
   a. sole-support pad and shoe
   b. deep-seated bar shoe
   c. wide-web reverse shoe
   d. frog-support bar shoe

8. Severed deep flexor tendon below the pastern joint can be mechanically treated with a:
   a. heart bar
   b. straight bar
   c. patten bar with heart bar insert
   d. square toe with lateral trailer

9. An alar or wing fracture of the distal phalanx is mechanically treated by stabilizing the hoof with a:
   a. heart bar with toe clip
   b. straight bar with continuous rim or several clips
   c. egg bar with side clips at first nail holes
   d. three-point shoe with no clips

10. The person who is legally in charge in a therapeutic case where blood is present, regardless of the expertise of collaborators is:
    a. farrier
    b. trainer
    c. veterinarian
    d. barn manager

11. The ligament that is most superficial in the horse's leg is the:
    a. V ligament
    b. X ligament
    c. Y ligament
    d. Z ligament

12. The stay apparatus of the hind limb is activated by:
    a. muscle tension on peronius tertius
    b. a slight muscle tonus on triceps brachii
    c. a slight muscle tonus on tensor facia latae
    d. a slight muscle tonus of lacertus fibrosis

All answers are on the following page.

Key to Sample Questions

Student/Apprentice Level

1.	a	7.	c
2.	b	8.	c
3.	c	9.	d
4.	b	10.	a
5.	b	11.	c
6.	b	12.	d

Beginning Farrier Level

1.	3	7.	d
2.	a	8.	b
3.	c	9.	a
4.	a	10.	c
5.	d	11.	c
6.	b	12.	d
		13.	a

Working Farrier Level

1.	a	7.	a
2.	c	8.	c
3.	d	9.	a
4.	b	10.	c
5.	d	11.	d
6.	a	12.	d

Advanced Farrier Level

1.	c	7.	d
2.	a	8.	c
3.	b	9.	b
4.	c	10.	c
5.	d	11.	c
6.	b	12.	c

Appendix 4

Standards of Farriery
Assessment Sheet

Appendix 4

Standards of Farriery Assessment Sheet

When the candidate meets the standard described to the examiners' satisfaction, circle YES. A YES does not mean there is no room for improvement. If the standard is not attained or only partly met, circle NO.

1. Trimming

Circle YES or NO   *Standards for Evaluating Trimming*

10	Yes	or	No	Toe/Heel Balance – dressed hoof toe and dorsal surface of distal phalanx parallel to front of pastern, when viewed from the side – exceptions approved by examiner. (Examples: Underrun heels or club foot.)

10   Yes   or   No   Toe/Heel Balance – dressed hoof toe and dorsal surface of distal phalanx parallel to front of pastern, when viewed from the side – exceptions approved by examiner. (Examples: Underrun heels or club foot.)

10   Yes   or   No   Medial/Lateral Balance – hoof ground surface perpendicular to pastern and/or leg axis, when viewed from in front.

10   Yes   or   No   Hoof Form Balance – foot dressed around its center to correspond to shape of distal phalanx and coronary band.

10   Yes   or   No   Wall straight from upper one-third of hoof – flares dressed, not dubbed.

5   Yes   or   No   Sole not bearing weight with no more than 1/8" of sole and the white line level with wall.

5   Yes   or   No   Wall ground surface a flat, but not necessarily continuous, bearing surface.

5   Yes   or   No   Frog is left healthy and easy to clean. Where shaped, corresponds to sensitive frog.

5   Yes   or   No   Bar bearing level with wall for width of shoe. Bars left strong.

10   Yes   or   No   Sole has shape of bottom of distal phalanx and does not yield to thumb pressure.

70 TOTAL

2. Shoe Making or Preparation

Circle YES or NO   *Standards for Evaluating Shoes*

5   Yes or No   Nail holes all in a safe position – width of dressed wall from edge – nail holes are parallel to white line.

5   Yes or No   Nail holes all in a safe position – forward of widest part of foot or front half of shoe (holes not to be used are nail-riveted closed).

5   Yes or No   Nails appropriate to foot fit in nail holes – flush push tight with pitch varied to angle of wall.

5   Yes or No   Inside foot shoe face seated out (sole relief) – determined with ruler on shoe foot surface (1/8" inside of nail holes to inside edge).

5   Yes or No   Level wall and bar contact (determined with ruler on shoe) – foot surface 1/8" inside of nail holes to outside edge and quarters (heels) of shoe level.

5   Yes or No   Heel form – straight, beveled, safed or boxed as required by examiner.

5   Yes or No   Clip blends in with flow of shoe (if no clip required, mark Yes).

10   Yes or No   Toe balanced and forged uniformly from toe to heel. Shoe has form or symmetry and flows, supporting the limb without sharp bends.

3   Yes or No   Clip(s) uniform height and thickness (if no clip required, mark Yes).

2   Yes or No   Shoe free of deep hammer marks and/or fire damage.

50 TOTAL

3. Shoe Fitting to Foot

Circle YES or NO   *Standards for Evaluating Shoe Fitting*

10   Yes   or   No   Shoe has form or symmetry that improves the foot (without sharp bends). Foot surface follows outline of hoof wall until after the last nail holes where it may be wider than the hoof to accommodate limb conformation.

5   Yes   or   No   Shoe heels are off the frog and cover all of the buttresses.

10   Yes   or   No   Shoe heels end 1/8" behind the buttresses and are fit full from zero at widest part of hoof to 1/16" at heels except where allowance has been made for limb conformation – exceptions approved by examiner.

2   Yes   or   No   Shoe is boxed on foot surface edge to the foot at broken places and at heels or where allowance has been made for limb conformation.

10   Yes   or   No   Tight union between shoe and hoof with no farrier-created spaces between them. No eased heels.

5   Yes   or   No   Nail holes positioned over outside of white line in front half of foot.

3   Yes   or   No   Shoe heels are finished smooth to correspond to heel shape.

5   Yes   or   No   Shoe is centered on the foot.

5   Yes   or   No   No sole pressure. No more than 1/8" sole contact. Seat of corn contact is reduced.

5   Yes   or   No   Clip fits flush into wall (if no clip required, mark Yes).

60 TOTAL

4. Nailing and Finishing

Circle YES or NO   *Standards for Evaluating Nailing and Finishing*

10   Yes or No   Nails are all safe – no evidence of close nailing when tested with hoof testers.

10   Yes or No   Nails exit about one-third of the way up the hoof wall at the heel nail. Nail line rises toward the toe or is parallel to shoe and close to a straight line.

5   Yes or No   Nail heads seat evenly into the shoe with about 1/16" protruding from the shoe and free from distortion.

5   Yes or No   Clinches are all uniform in size and nearly square.

2   Yes or No   Clinches are all set into the wall and strong (thick).

3   Yes or No   Wall is free of deep rasp marks and grooves under the clinches.

3   Yes or No   The entire job is polished and smooth.

2   Yes or No   Clinches are all perpendicular to the shoe or all perpendicular to the coronary band.

40 TOTAL

Possible Points: 220   **Score** _____   **Failed**

Passing Percentage _____

Actual Percentage _____ **Passed**

Stopped (circle one): Cut too deep, out of balance more than 1/4", quicked with a nail, lame, out of time

Examiner _____   Foot Condition: Poor Fair Good

Examinee _____   Horse Behavior: Poor Fair Good

Date _____

Appendix 5

Gene Autry's Cowboy Code

Appendix 5

Gene Autry's Cowboy Code

"Over the years I have taken some ribbing about my cowboy's Code, the set of rules I evolved to govern the role of the western hero. They must sound naïve to today's do-your-own-thing disciples. But we took such matters seriously then and the code tapped a spirit that was alive in the land. It went like this:

1. The cowboy must never shoot first, hit a smaller man or take unfair advantage.

2. He must never go back on his word, or a trust confided in him.

3. He must always tell the truth.

4. He must be gentle with children, the elderly, and animals.

5. He must not advocate or possess radical or religiously intolerant ideas.

6. He must help people in distress.

7. He must be a good worker.

8. He must keep himself clean in thought, speech, action, and personal habits.

9. He must respect women, parents, and the laws of the nation.

10. The cowboy is a patriot.

"Under this code, some have said, the cowboy became a sort of adult boy scout. Maybe so. I am aware that sophisticated people might snicker at such sentiments. But I didn't exactly move in sophisticated circles. I never felt there was anything wrong with striving to be better than you are."

Reprinted from the May 1978 issue of *Rodeo News*, pp. 30, 33

The Scout Law

1. A Scout is Trustworthy

A Scout's honor is to be trusted. If he were to violate his honor by telling a lie, or by cheating, or by not doing exactly a given task, when trusted on his honor, he may be directed to hand over his Scout Badge.

2. A Scout is Loyal

He is loyal to all to whom loyalty is due, his Scout leader, his home, and parents and country.

3. A Scout is Helpful

He must be prepared at any time to save life, help injured persons, and share the home duties. He must do at least one "Good Turn" to somebody every day.

4. A Scout is Friendly

He is a friend to all and a brother to every other Scout.

5. A Scout is Courteous

He is polite to all, especially to women, children, old people and the weak and helpless. He must not take pay for being helpful or courteous.

6. A Scout is Kind

He is a friend to animals. He will not kill nor hurt any living creature needlessly but will strive to save and protect all harmless life.

7. A Scout is Obedient

He obeys his parents, Scoutmaster, Patrol Leader, and all other duly constituted authorities.

8. A Scout is Cheerful

He smiles whenever he can. His obedience to orders is prompt and cheery. He never shirks nor grumbles at hardships.

9. A Scout is Thrifty

He does not wantonly destroy property. He works faithfully, wastes nothing, and makes the best use of his opportunities. He saves his money so that he may pay his own way, be generous to those in need, and helpful to worthy objects. He may work for pay, but must not receive tips for courtesies or Good Turns.

10. A Scout is Brave

He has the courage to face danger in spite of fear, and to stand up for the right against the coaxing of friends or the jeers or threats of enemies, and defeat does not down him.

11. A Scout is Clean

He keeps clean in body and thought, stands for clean speech, clean sport, clean habits, and travels with a clean crowd.

12. A Scout is Reverent

He is reverent toward God. He is faithful in his religious duties, and respects the convictions of others in matters of custom and religion.

References

Six-Figure Shoeing

References

Albrecht, S. *Service, Service, Service*. Adams Media Corp., Holbrook, MA, 1994.

Allen, J. *As a Man Thinketh*. DeVoiss and Co., 1983.

Allen, K. *Time and Information Management that Really Works*. Out of Print

Allen, N. Building a Farrier Business Plan. *Footnotes* 3 (3):20, 1994.

Arkebauer, J. B. *Golden Entrepreneuring*. McGraw-Hill, New York, 1995.

Autry, G. The Cowboy Code. *Rodeo News*, May, 1978.

Bangs, D. and A. Axman. *Launching Your Home Based Business*. Upstart Publishing Co. Chicago, 1998.

Boden, E. (Editor). Burns inquiry into hunting: the NAFBAE evidence. *The Forge*, April 2000.

Boy Scouts of America. *Handbook for Boys*. Boy Scouts of America, New Brunswick, NJ, 1948.

Bradford, R. *A Teacher's Quest*. Brigham Young University Press, Provo, UT, 1971.

Burg, B. *Endless Referrals*. McGraw-Hill, New York, 1998.

Carnegie, D. *How to Win Friends and Influence People*. Simon and Schuster, New York, 1981.

Cathcart, J. *The Acorn Principle*. St. Martin's Press, New York, 1998.

Cialdini, R. B. *Influence: The Psychology of Persuasion*. Quill – William Morrow and Co., New York, 1993.

Classen, G. *The Richest Man in Babylon*. New American Library, 1997.

Collins, H. *Shedding the Blinkers*. Post Graduate Foundation, University of Sydney, Sydney, Australia, 1997.

Corson, L., G. Hadley and C. Stevens. *The Secrets of Super Selling*. Berkley Books, New York, 1991.

Covey, S. R. *Living the Seven Habits*. Simon and Schuster, New York, 1999.

Covey, S. R. *The Seven Habits of Highly Effective People*. Simon and Schuster, New York, 1989.

Clark, D. *Puppies for Sale and Other Inspirational Tales*. Health Communications, Inc., Deerfield Beach, FL, 1997.

Crandall, R. (Editor*). Marketing For People Not in Marketing*. Select Press, Corte Madera, CA, 1998.

Daniels, B. B. *Sunday on the Farm*. St. Eloy Publ., Cascade, MD, 1995.

Dooley, D. Lifestyle Concerns of the Practitioner. *Proceedings of The American Association of Equine Practitioners*, 1991

Emerson, R. W. *Essays*. A. L. Burt Co. Boston, MA, 1841.

Farriers Registration Council. *Farriers Craft and Business Guide*, FRC, London, 1998.

Frankl, V. E. *Man's Search For Meaning*. Washington Square Press. New York, 1984.

Gerber, M. E. *The E Myth Revisited*. Harper Business, New York, 1995.

Girard, J. *How to Sell Anything to Anybody*. Warner Books. New York. 1977.

Grandin, T. *Thinking in Pictures*. Random House, New York, 1995.

Guage, L. and N. Guage. *If Wishes Were Horses*. St. Martin's Press, New York, 1995.

Guest, E. A. *Collected Verse of Edgar A. Guest*. The Reilly & Lee Co., Chicago, 1938.

Hammond, D. J. (Editor). *The Fine Art of Doing Better*. American Motivational Assoc., Scottsdale, AZ, 1974.

Hartman, T. *The Color Code*. Color Code Unlimited, Salt Lake City, 1987.

Heymering, H. *On the Horse's Foot and Shoeing*. St. Eloy Publ., Cascade, MD, 1990.

Hill, N. *Think and Grow Rich*. Napoleon Hill Foundation, Niles, IL, 1960.

Johnson, G. G. *In The Balance*. Pica, Golden, CO, 1993.

Kersey, C. *Unstoppable*. Sourcebooks, Inc., Naperville, IL, 1998.

Ketchum, R. M. *Will Rogers*. American Heritage Publ. Co., New York, 1973.

Kiyosaki, R.T. and S.L Lechter. *Rich Dad Poor Dad*. Warner Books, New York, 1998.

Kiyosaki, R.T. and S.L. Lechter. *The Cash Flow Quadrant*. Tech Press, Inc., Paradise Valley, AZ, 1999.

LeBoeuf, M. *How to Win Customers and Keep Them For Life*. Berkley Books, New York, 1987.

LeBoeuf, M. *The Perfect Business*. Simon and Schuster, New York, 1996.

LeBoeuf, M. *Working Smart*. Warner Books, New York. 1979.

Levoy, R. P. *The $100,000 Practice and How to Build It*. Prentice-Hall, Englewood Cliffs, NJ, 1966.

Linkletter, A. *I Didn't Do It Alone: The Autobiography of Art Linkletter*. Out of Print.

Mackay, H. *Pushing the Envelope*. Ballantine Books, New York, 1999.

Mackay, H. *Sharkproof*. Harper Business, New York, 1993.

Mandino, O. *The Greatest Secret in the World*. Bantam Books, New York, 1972.

Mattinson, A. B. *Hunting's Art of Horseshoeing*. Bailliere, Tindall and Cox, London, 1922.

Milani, M. *The Art of Veterinary Practice: A Guide to Client Communications*. University of Pennsylvania Press, Philadelphia, 1995.

Miller, L. F. Developing Client Relationships. *Equine Practice*, 21:1, Jan. 1999.

Miller, R. M. The Relationship Between Veterinarian and Horse Owner. *The Western Horseman*, July, 1982.

Miller, R. M. Understanding the Horse Owner. *Equine Veterinary Science*. 9:6, Nov/Dec 1989.

Mitchell, B. *Bet on Cowboys, Not Horses*. York, Shaker Heights, OH, 1993.

Nightingale, E. *The Strangest Secret in The World*. (Audio) Nightingale-Conant Corp., Niles, IL, 1972.

Osborne, C. A. The Human Side of Veterinary Medicine. How can each of us be trustworthy? *Journal of the American Veterinary Medical Association*, 203:10, Nov. 15, 1993.

Pavia, A. A Solid Background and Continuing Education Are Key to a Successful Practice. *Equine Practice*, 22:2, Feb. 2000.

Pine, B. J. and J. H. Gilmore. *The Experience Economy*. Harvard Business School Press, Boston, MA, 1999.

Prince, L. *The Farrier and His Craft*. J. A. Allen, London, 1980.

Reeves, R. *Reality in Advertising*. Out of Print.

Reid, O. L. (Editor). *Franklin's Autobiography*. American Book Co., New York, 1910.

Rhode, N. *The Gift of Family*. Thomas Nelson Publ., Nashville, TN, 1991.

Ries, A. and J. Trout. *Bottom-Up Marketing*. McGraw-Hill, New York, 1989.

Ries, A. and L. Ries. *The 22 Immutable Laws of Branding*. Harper Business, New York, 1998.

Ries, A. *Focus*. Harper Business, New York, 1996.

Schreiner, O. *The Story of an African Farm*. Dover Publ., New York, 1998.

Schuller, R. H. *Move Ahead with Possibility Thinking*. Spire Books, Old Tappan, NJ, 1967.

Sellnow, L. Getting a Second Opinion. *The Horse*, Feb, 2000.

Sharpe, R. and D. Lewis. *The Success Factor*. Warner Books, New York, 1977.

Sinetar, M. *Do What You Love, The Money Will Follow*. Dell, New York, 1987.

Sinetar, M. *To Build The Life You Want, Create the Work You Love*. St. Martin's Griffin, New York, 1995.

Smith, H. W. *The 10 Natural Laws of Successful Time and Life Management*. Warner Books, New York, 1994.

Smithcors, J. F. *The Veterinarian in America 1625 – 1975*. American Veterinary Publ., Santa Barbara, CA, 1975.

Stern, L. Raise Your Rates. *Home Office Computing*, Sept., 1996.

Stoll, C. *Silicon Snake Oil*. Anchor Books, New York, 1995.

Sykes, C. *Dumbing Down Our Kids*. St. Martin's, Griffin, NY, 1995.

Teplitz, J.V. *Switched-On Living*. Hampton Road Publ., Norfolk, VA, 1994.

Trout, J. *The New Positioning*. McGraw-Hill, New York, 1996.

Trout, J. and S. Rivkin. *The Power of Simplicity*. McGraw-Hill, New York, 1998.

Waitley, D. *The New Dynamics of Winning*. Quill – William Morrow and Co., New York, 1995.

Wilson, J. *Word of Mouth Marketing*. John Wiley and Sons, New York, 1994.

Wutchiett, C. R. *What is a Well-Managed Practice?* Wutchiett and Associates, Inc., Columbus, OH, 1998.

Ziglar, Z. *See You At The Top*. Pelican, Gretna, LA, 1977.

Frequently Consulted Periodicals

American Farriers Journal
American Horse Council Tax Letter
Anvil
Equus
Footnotes Newsletter
Horse Foot Care and Lameness
Proceedings of the American Association of Equine Practitioners
The Forge (from Great Britain)
The Horse
The Journal of Animal Science
The Journal of the American Veterinary Medical Association
The Readers Digest
The Wall Street Journal
The Western Horseman
USA Today – The Coloradoan

Index

Index